# THE MR. THANK YOU

## PROJECT

A journey to elevate the level
of gratitude on the planet...

*one card at a time.*

## JOHN ISRAEL

ISBN-13 (Print/Paperback) 978-0-9971283-2-1

ISBN-13 (PDF version) 978-0-9971283-3-8

Cover: Rebecca Feldbush

Page design: Justin Oefelein

Contact John Israel at email: John@MrThankYou.com or visit the
website: www.MrThankYou.com

# Table of Contents

## Section 2: EMOTIONAL INTELLIGENCE AND GRATITUDE

## Section 3: GRATITUDE AND COMMUNITY

## Section 4: THE ROI OF GRATITUDE

I dedicate this book to my wife Monica, and boys Anderson and Rohn. You are my source of inspiration to do good in the world.

# Foreword

The one thing about being diagnosed with cancer is you find out who your true friends are.

In November 2016, at 38 years old, married to the woman of my dreams and with two young children, I was rushed to the hospital Emergency Room with difficulty breathing. As someone who lives a very healthy lifestyle, I was surprised and confused to find out that my lung had collapsed, my kidneys were failing, and my heart was dangerously close to heart failure.

I was quickly diagnosed with a very rare, aggressive form of leukemia. The week before, I was fine. And now I'm being told that this particular cancer is so rare and aggressive, that the best my Oncologist could give me was a terrifying 10 percent chance of surviving. Or for those "glass-is-half-empty" folks, I was given a 90 percent chance of dying.

This happened just one month before I was scheduled to host 300+ attendees at our annual Best Year Ever Blueprint (BYEB) live experience/event, where people from around the world fly to San Diego, California, and we map out the next year of their lives to be the best one yet.

I, on the other hand, was about to enter into what would prove to be the most difficult year of my life.

Thankfully I was able to trust my business partner, Jon Berghoff, to run the event while I immediately began undergoing one of the most intensive chemotherapy treatments available.

While I had to spend that time really taking care of myself, I was blown away by the support of friends. It cost us tens of thousands of dollars to fight this cancer (and over

$1,000,000 from our insurance provider). Nearly every dollar we spent was recovered by generous donations from friends and business associates.

Precisely one year later, I'm given the "clear" that my cancer has gone into remission. While there are many things to celebrate, one of those is that I'll be able to be present for this year's Best Year Ever Blueprint event that I had to miss with my original diagnosis. It meant so much to see and appreciate all my loyal clients, friends, and fans who stuck by me during that challenging time.

I've been fortunate to call John Israel a friend for over a decade, and our families have also become very close.

I knew very little about what John was up to except that he had been writing a lot of thank you cards. I still remember reading the one he sent me between hospital visits.

There was a lot of good buzz going around his Mr. Thank You Project, so we invited him to speak at our BYEB event.

What ensued showed me the true heart of John Israel. I would be the recipient of what he coined as a "Communal Gratitude Experience."

During two days of our three-day event, John coordinated with 300+ participants to write letters of appreciation for not only me, but every member of my family: my mother, Julie, who witnessed her child almost die (for a second time); my father, Mark, who went with me to every chemo treatment although he lived in another state; and my wife, Ursula, who played both mom and dad to our children while we went through the hardest time of our lives together.

At the end of John's very powerful message, a participant stands up and asks for a microphone. The next thing you know, my father, who is sitting next to me, is receiving one of the most powerful acknowledgments of his life from someone he hardly knows. A standing ovation erupts, and we run over to give this man a hug.

Then another participant stands up to read a letter to my mother empathizing about how hard it must have been for her to watch her only son so close to death. Another eruption of applause.

The cherry on top is when my best friend, Jeremy, stands up and reads two letters. One to me and one to my wife, Ursula. He shares how important our friendship is and how grateful he is for my recovery. There isn't a dry eye in the house (mine included).

Just when we think it's over, overwhelmed with positive emotions, John invites my entire family on stage to give us a public acknowledgment. He then bestows me, my wife, and parents with a stack of letters from the participants who share their thoughts of love, gratitude, and appreciation.

All this was coordinated by John, and he pulled it off right in front of me without me knowing.

Not only did he transform my family with this abundantly generous act, but he transformed the environment of that entire conference. Our community still talks about it as one of the highlights of their entire experience. I have been to a lot of events and conventions, but I have NEVER seen or experienced anything like this.

We wound up hiring John to consult with our coaching organization about how we can implement thank you cards and gratitude into our business process.

I'm grateful to call John Israel a friend. After reading this book, I'm sure you'll consider him a friend too.

*John Israel is truly changing the world with the Mr. Thank You Project, and I'm excited to see how your world changes after reading this book.*

    *–Hal Elrod*

The Mr. Thank You Project

# Read This First

I am not a very grateful person by nature. I believe few of us are. Gratitude is distinct from happiness for this reason.

You don't need to teach a three year old child to be happy, but you do need to teach them to say, "thank you."

Ever seen a kid at play? Then you've seen happiness. Ever hear someone say, *Wow, that's a grateful kid over there?* Not as commonly. Why?

Gratitude requires perspective, and perspective takes time. It's part of the maturation process. Even as we get older it's still a challenge.

Society is moving ever faster and our ability to be grateful is having difficulty catching up. It's hard to appreciate what you have when the new 2.0 version just came out.

I believe that gratitude is like a muscle, the more you work on it, the stronger it gets and the easier it is to access.

The Mr. Thank You Project was a personal, social experiment to see how far I could push myself with gratitude, which I realize is a statement you've probably never heard before.

By a big stroke of luck, and part due to my joy for story telling, I've been blessed to share the Mr. Thank You Project with millions of listeners and viewers of television news outlets, on-line blogs, print magazines, radio shows, podcasts, and just about any other form of media out there.

Almost more than the project itself, what inspires me every day is discovering how many people started following suit with their own Mr. (or Ms.) Thank You Projects.

It turns out gratitude is contagious.

Based on the feedback of fans, followers, and practitioners, I laid out some specific challenges through out this book for you to workout that "gratitude muscle". Some activities will be fun and easy, while others might be out of your comfort zone.

While you can gain a lot of value from merely reading this book, keep in mind that the best version of yourself lives at the end of your comfort zone.

If at any point you say, "Geez, he did what? I would never do that. But I would do (some lighter version)?" then I did my job.

I would never invite you to do something that I haven't or am not willing to do myself.

While I want this book to be an entertaining and enjoyable read, I also want you to experience it. At the end of various sections I put action steps to take. You don't have to do them, yet if you do, I think you'll notice the positive benefits of flexing that gratitude muscle.

At the end of this book is an invitation to participate in a 30-day Mr. Thank You challenge. Feel free to go to **www.MrThankYou.com/30** for more information, and join our Facebook community where people from all over the world share tips, challenges, and breakthroughs of their own personal gratitude projects.

What gets me excited is that Mr. Thank You isn't just about Mr. Thank You. It's about being an example for the world to see what happens when you commit to embodying your highest values every day.

Curious to see what that result is? Then read on my friend. We've got a wild ride ahead of us.

# Introduction

On October 10th, 2016, I started the Mr. Thank You Project, a global movement to inspire 74 million thank you cards written all over the world. I kicked it off by writing five thank you cards every day for an entire year.

Now as the reader, I imagine this brings up a lot of questions. The first of which: WHY?

It all began with an unforeseen promise I made to myself right out of college when I was at a very high and also a very low point in my life.

I was 24 years old and had just begun my personal growth journey.

I was one of the top sales people in the country for the Cutco Corporation, a 60+ year- old housewares company based out of upstate New York.

What started as a summer job selling kitchen knives as a 19-year-old college student, had turned into a lucrative career opportunity that helped me pay for school and become financially independent at a young age. But I was ready for change.

I had just doubled my biggest sales year and was inducted into the company's Hall of Fame for my performance and contributions.

I lived in Santa Barbara, California, at the time, and decided to attend a personal development seminar called the Landmark Forum that I hoped would give me some direction in the next stages of my life.

While many things were said and taught in that seminar, there was one lesson that I was left with:

*Inside every life experience, there is a gift. Your job is to find it.*

As simple as it may sound, that lesson had a profound impact on me. While yes, I was successful financially, I was broken emotionally.

What drove me to be a hard worker was that I didn't grow up with much. My family wasn't poor, but my parents valued education so highly that they spent all their money putting their five kids through private school (kindergarten through senior year of high school). I was the youngest in the family.

The interesting challenge of that private school education was that, while I did get good grades, I was surrounded by a lot of kids whose parents gave them everything. While some kids got brand new BMWs for their birthdays, I still remember the embarrassment of borrowing money from my track coach just to purchase my letterman jacket.

My parents did their best and promised to support me through college. Unfortunately, we all had the rug pulled out from under us when my father was diagnosed with Parkinson's disease while I was still in high school. He was the sole breadwinner in the family, and aside from the fear of what he and now the family would be dealing with, my chances of going to college were dwindling.

Fortunately, with a little family savings, and some scholarship money that came through, I made it through my freshman year of college at Gonzaga University. However, it would be up to me to make it back a second year.

I did everything from picking up that summer Cutco sales job, working as a lab aide on campus, being a resident assistant in the dorms, and I even walked in to the financial aid office to negotiate more scholarship money.

This experience caused me to grow up quickly, but not without a chip on my shoulder. I always felt like I needed to work a little harder than everyone else for what I had.

I harbored a lot of resentment during that time. I loved my dad, but I was angry that he missed most of my childhood because he traveled for his job simply to make ends meet at home.

During the Landmark Forum, I was able to find the gift in that experience. While yes, it was frustrating and challenging to grow up so quickly, it also drove me to be successful and more independent than a lot of people my age.

There was a lot to be grateful for in my life.

A few days after that personal development seminar, I found myself at 6 in the morning, sitting in my parked car at the beach in Santa Barbara. I was journaling as I often do every morning, but rather than venting about my struggles, all that came out was gratitude.

I thought about the times in my life and noticed that those moments when I grew the most occurred during my greatest challenges and weaknesses. Whether it was my track coach who had the means and candor to buy me my letterman jacket without making me feel indebted, or my parents who couldn't support me financially but made sure to let me know that I was always loved and going to do big things with my life.

All the challenges in my life took on a new meaning because I realized, for the first time in my life, that everything needed to happen exactly as it happened for me to be where I was in that moment. Everything had a purpose.

I began to appreciate 'me,' and everyone who made 'me' possible.

I drove home and started sending email after email to the people who had impacted my life: mentors, teachers, coaches, family, friends.

Of course, I made sure to call my mom and dad and thank them for all the sacrifices they made for their kids and let them know that their investment was worthwhile.

With each message I sent, or call that I made, that gratitude inside me grew and grew. Before long, people started reaching back to tell me how appreciative they were to hear of their impact on me.

I began to cry. Not the tears of a broken heart, but the tears of an open heart. Nothing mattered more than acknowledging and appreciating everyone in my life.

I was on such a high of gratitude, I remember telling myself: "If I could feel like this every day of my life, I could die happy."

Thus begot the question: "Is it truly possible to live every day with a grateful heart?"

What I didn't realize back then was how this question planted a seed in my mind that would blossom into my life's work.

## Start with WHY:

Ten years later, I had become a gratitude salesman. Seriously! It's a thing.

As a profession, I helped people say, "Thank you." Specifically, I had become a corporate gifting consultant representing my original employer, Cutco, and a few other high-quality brands.

Essentially this put me at real estate conferences, trade shows, and business expos where I'd speak and teach people how to express appreciation with their clients and employees to strengthen relationships and grow their businesses. Ultimately, this led clients to buy large quantities of the brands I represented as "thank you" gifts.

I was now married to my wife, Monica. We had a two-year-old son, and another child on the way.

We lived in Santa Maria, California, at the time, the midway point between Los Angeles and San Francisco.

Life was expanding rapidly.

In a very short time, we purchased our first home, started our family, and my wife left her job to become a stay-at-home mom. While these were all mutual decisions we made together, I started feeling the stress of becoming the sole provider.

I didn't want to let anyone down, so I buried myself in work. My 60-70-hour work weeks were normal, and my travel schedule put me all over the country on any given week of the month.

It was wearing on my life, my marriage, and ultimately—my business began to suffer as well. Working just to make ends meet was depressing.

Personal development books, seminars, and coaching had become a regular part of my life at this point. I always appreciated the perspective others could give who had similar life experiences or challenges and had come through on the other side.

Everything changed one day when I came upon a TED Talk by Simon Sinek called "Start with Why."

Simon's message was simple yet profound: "People don't care what you do, they care why you are doing it. In business, people don't buy what you sell, they buy why you're selling it. If you want to change your life and business, start with WHY."

It got me thinking: "What's my WHY?"

I was so caught up simply trying to provide for my family that I hadn't stopped to think about the end game. What was the purpose of it all?

I wanted to find a why so big that it would inspire me, inspire my clients, and inspire the world.

I spent a few days pondering that question and then an idea hit me. It was way back from my freshman biology class in college.

The professor was talking about the vastness of the world's oceans. Trillions and trillions of gallons of water everywhere.

He asked the class, "How much energy would it take to elevate the temperature of every body of water on the planet by 1 degree (Celsius or Fahrenheit)?" No one raised a hand.

"A lot," he said. We chuckled. Of course, he then gave us the actual number that I do not recall, but it was big. More than any one fish, one person, or one country could create.

I was struck by this concept and thought, "What could make such a big impact?"

The teacher launched into a speech about global warming issues, and how *collective neglect* was having an adverse effect on the planet.

While his speech did motivate me to become an avid recycler, his "1 degree" concept really stuck with me.

I started to think, "If a 1-degree temperature difference could have such a negative impact, what about a 1-degree difference with gratitude?"

At the current time, with 7.4 billion people on the planet, 1 percent of the world's population is 74 million people.

Could I do something that would start a ripple that would positively impact 1 percent of the world's population with gratitude?

I didn't know the answer, but the question got me excited.

## Start with YOU!

I consulted my business coach Ben from Epic Impact, a coaching and consulting firm out of San Francisco.

I shared with Ben my excitement about impacting 1 percent of the world's population with gratitude. While he liked the valiant nature of the mission, Ben asked me a very poignant question and shared a story that would uncover the next steps on my journey.

Ben: Did I ever tell you about the story of the man who tried to change the world?
Me: No.

Ben: The story goes like this:

> *When I was a young man, I wanted to change the world.*
>
> *I found it was difficult to change the world, so I tried to change my nation.*
>
> *When I found I couldn't change the nation, I began to focus on my town. I couldn't change the town, and as an older man, I tried to change my family.*
>
> *Now, as an old man, I realize the only thing I can change is myself, and suddenly I realize that if long ago I had changed myself, I could have made an impact on my family. My family and I could have made an impact on our town. Their impact could have changed the nation and I could indeed have changed the world.*

**—Unknown Monk 1100 A.D.**

Ben: My question to you is this: How can you embody gratitude at such a high level in your own life that you inspire it in others? Because if you want to change the world, it starts with YOU.

I sat with Ben's question for a few days. "How can I embody gratitude?" I thought.

Charles Duhigg's book, *The Power of Habit*, came to mind. Charles talks about people changing their lives by changing their habits. The most powerful of which he calls "keystone habits," which are habits that have a multiplying positive effect in our lives.

Making your bed in the morning, for example, is a habit that Duhigg states will make you more productive, have a greater sense of well-being, and better budgeting skills. When we perform this simple two-minute habit, we are starting the day by bringing order to our lives, and it trickles down from there.

What habit around gratitude could I perform that could have such a compounding effect?

While I had tried to start many good habits throughout my life, I realized a trend that the best habits I had created in my life always fit a three-point criteria. For it to stick, the habit needed to be: simple, duplicatable, and effective.

The more complex the habit or change I wanted to make, the harder it will be to honor. To become healthier, instead of changing my sleep habits, eating habits, and exercise routine, I needed to find ONE THING I could change and stick with. This is also important because, in lining up my actions with the big WHY of elevating the level of gratitude on the planet, I wanted the habit to be something that others would be inspired by and easily able to implement in their own lives.

I also found that a daily habit, not just something I did once a week or month, was most effective. If I could perform the habit every day, it was more likely to be taken over by the subconscious mind and I had to think about it less and less to perform it. Take brushing your teeth, for example. I rarely have to think about it because I brush the first thing in the morning and the last thing before I go to bed. I don't have to convince myself or set an alarm. I just do it.

Lastly, the actions needed to produce a result that is consistent with my goals. Duhigg calls this "reward." When we get a reward, we are encouraged to perform the activity again and again. For example, if my goal is to lose weight and the habit I pick up is weightlifting, I may or may not hit that goal because weightlifting can be more conducive to gaining muscle mass than losing weight. A cardio regimen is a pivotal part of most weight-loss programs because it burns fat more quickly than trying to bench press heavy amounts of weight.

I thought, "What's a habit I can create that is simple, duplicatable, effective, and replicable that would also positively elevate my own level of gratitude and that of others?"

While it seemed like a tall order, an idea popped into my head.

## Thank You Cards:

Two years ago when my wife, Monica, had just given birth to our first son, Anderson, she was taking an online personal development program called "The Wisdom Course."

One day the instructor was talking about the concept of abundance. He asked the participants, "If you want more abundance in your life, look at what you have an abundance of, and give it away."

Unbeknownst to me, Monica had a habit of purchasing cute or thoughtful thank you cards whenever she was out at a department store. She had amassed a collection of over 100 such cards and realized that she hadn't sent any of them out. So that's what she decided to do.

For the next two months, quite literally with a nursing baby in one arm, Monica wrote thank you card after thank you card to her family, close friends, distant friends she hadn't spoken with in years, and old work associates. In total she sent over 60 cards in the course of 40 days.

What amazed me was the intentionality and personalization that Monica gave to every card. None of them was the same. For her uncle with five boys, she didn't write one card for the whole family. She wrote six cards, one for each person. The cards recalled her favorite moments with each of them and, for the younger boys, how much she loved watching them grow up.

As a new mom, even with all the hormonal changes, lack of sleep, and new responsibilities, Monica had become more gracious and loving than I had ever experienced. She was also getting so much love back from her community with text messages, emails, and phone calls from people thanking Monica for her authentic appreciation. She was definitely being and experiencing an abundance of gratitude.

"What might happen if I committed to writing thank you cards for 365 consecutive days?" I thought. "What if I committed an entire year to exploring my capacity to experience and express gratitude with handwritten notes?"

It hit all the habit parameters I was looking for.

Thank you cards are simple. It's not complex to buy some stationery and write down what you appreciate about someone. You can even use a generic piece of paper or a napkin if you have to.

Thank you cards are duplicatable. It wouldn't take much time, and—important to my travel schedule—it would be something that I could do from anywhere.

Thank you cards are also clearly effective. From my experience of sending all those gratitude emails, and from seeing how writing all those cards affected my wife, I knew it was something that had the ability to raise my level of gratitude.

## The Game and the Rules:

I shared these ideas with my coach Ben, and he told me, "I like the idea. But we want to get really specific about this commitment. Think of it like a game. How do you win, how do you lose, and what are the rules? How many cards will you write every day and what are the consequences if you miss a day?"

I took a few more days to think about his questions. How many cards should I write?

One card every day seemed doable, but didn't inspire me and I didn't know if it would inspire others either.

Ten cards every day seemed a little too extreme. I didn't know how good they would be if I had to write 10 thank you cards every day.

What about five? Five ... five cards every day would be hard, but it would be doable and I thought it would challenge me to grow, and might inspire others to make gratitude a habit.

Ben and I reconvened on the ideas of my project.

I told Ben, "I'm going to write five thank you cards every day for an entire year." "Sounds great," he said. "How do you win or lose, and what are the rules?"

I gave him the list:

## RULE 1) ALL NOTES MUST BE HANDWRITTEN.

It would be easy for me to copy and paste a similar thank you email multiple times, but it would be less impactful. I felt that handwriting was so rare and would be more valuable to people.

## RULE 2) EVERY DAY FIVE CARDS MUST BE WRITTEN. AND EVERY MORNING STARTS AT ZERO.

Meaning, I can't wait until Sunday and write 35 thank you cards so that I average five per day. If this is going to be an action that forces me into the emotional state of gratitude every day, then it's an activity that must be done daily.

## RULE 3) A MAXIMUM OF THREE CARDS COUNT PER INDIVIDUAL.

This means I can't write 365 cards to my wife and count them. I can only imagine her annoyance, "Listen, you don't need to write me a thank you card for going to the grocery store." The luster would be lost.

I can count up to three for any one person, and anything above that does not count toward the five-per-day challenge.

## RULE 4) WRITE LESS THAN FIVE THANK YOU CARDS IN A DAY; DONATE $100 TO CHARITY.

I needed to add some type of pain that would keep me accountable to following through and I thought donating money would be a valiant accountability tool.

"Add a zero," said Ben.

"Excuse me?" I replied. "What do you mean add a zero?" "Make it $1,000 if you miss a day."

Taken aback, I replied, "Why?"

Ben asked, "Are you probably going to donate a hundred or a couple hundred dollars to charity this year?"

"Yes," I said.

"Then it's not really a *pain*. You are setting yourself up to fail here. If this really matters to you, and you want to take this project seriously, I don't want you giving yourself an easy out to miss a day, and miss the opportunity to experience the impact of what you want to accomplish. If you have to donate $1,000 for every day you miss, how many days are you going to miss writing five cards this year?"

"None," I said confidently. "Great. Then add a zero."

I gulped. OK.

## RULE 4) WRITE LESS THAN FIVE THANK YOU CARDS IN A DAY; DONATE $1,000 TO CHARITY.

What did I just get myself into?

# Who?

I took another week to plan out how I was going to proceed with what became known as *The Mr. Thank You Project.*

I started by making a list of people I wanted to thank. There were several people I knew right away that I wanted to write an appreciative letter to: family, friends, clients, associates. After a few days of digging through my cell phone and social media friends, I had approximately 350 people on my list.

Herein lies the first challenge: When you scale five thank you cards every day for 365 days, that adds up to 1,825 cards.

"Where was I going to find these other 1,475 people to appreciate? Would I be able to find five people to thank every day for the next 365? Would I run out of people and owe $100,000 to charity at the end of this year?" These were my fears.

While I wasn't 100 percent sure of the answers, I was 100 percent committed that I would find a way, which most of us discover about ourselves when we set big goals with high levels of accountability.

I made my list, and I checked it twice. Not to find out who was naughty or nice, but to literally make sure I didn't put the same people on the list more than once, or God forbid forget my grandma. It would be an ever-growing, ever-changing list.

But now it was time to get started.

If you'd like to see a more comprehensive list of who I sent cards to, you can find it toward the back of this book in the section titled: My List. I started by tracking most everyone's name I wrote cards to via an Excel worksheet, but now we track everything through **www.MrThankYou. com.** You can set up a free portal there if you'd like.

# BECOMING A GOOD FINDER

"What you *appreciate*, **appreciates**."

–Lynne Twist

# Morgan's Card

The night before my project began, I could hardly sleep. Unfortunately, I still had a full day of work ahead of me.

I rolled out of bed extra early around 5:30 a.m. and drove to Starbucks to start writing my thank you cards.

While I expected to begin by writing to some of the people on my list, I began the drive by asking the question, *"Who am I going to thank today?"*

That question would be my guiding light this year.

I noticed myself being more observant of everyone and everything. I wanted to try and catch someone doing something good.

The first human being I interacted with that morning was named Morgan. She was my Starbucks barista. Even though it was now 5:45 in the morning, Morgan greeted me with a smile.

How can you do that? How can you be ready to go and smiling at people this early? "She will be card #1 of 1,825 in my year of thank you," I told myself.

At 6 a.m. I wrote this card and walked back up to the register to hand it to her. It reminded me of being a high school boy asking a girl to a dance. I was nervous, awkward, and my hands were sweating profusely.

I didn't wait around for her to read it, but I made sure to take a photo to document it. Thanks, Morgan. You started it all.

P.S. Make sure to read the P.S. at the bottom of the card.

Morgan

You get to be the first one in a year long journey of gratitude. It's strange, I get it. Getting a thank you card from the guy you filled up a thermos for... a complete stranger. None-the-less, here it goes.

Thank you for making my coffee. I'm sure you don't hear that enough. Thank you for picking up the heavy boxes to make sure we are stocked w/ sandwiches & pastries. Thank you for dealing w/ life as it is to show up here @ 5am w/ a smile on your face. I probably spend $1000+/year @ starbucks accross the country. Really no joke. I come back here all I call because you guys are great.

I committed the next year of my life to writing 5 Thank you cards per day, every day for 365 days. You get to be the first. I hope you feel special. because you are. Have an awesome day.

— John
Israel

P.S. I am totally married w/ a 2 year old and my wife is 8 months pregnant, so this is no way more than what it is... a Thank you. Just thought I'd throw that out there. LOL!

# What Is Gratitude?

As the project took flight, I decided to do some research that might help me deepen my understanding of the topic of gratitude.

*Gratitude, gratefulness, appreciation, thankful* are similar words I'll use interchangeably throughout this book.

It's nearly impossible to study the subject and not come across the work of Dr. Robert Emonns, professor of psychology at the University of California, Davis. He wrote the book on it. Actually, he's written four books on the topic of gratitude that I will refer to.

In his book, *Thanks* , Dr. Emmons says, "Gratefulness is the emotion we feel when given a gift, or noticing something as a gift. A gift given voluntarily and unexpectedly."

Think about the best gift you've ever been given. What was it? Was it something you asked for or was it a surprise? How did it make you feel?

For most people, the best gifts are the unexpected ones. They fill us with joy and excitement, and our natural response is to say, "Thank you."

In other words, they didn't have to give the gift, but they did. And because they did, the emotion called forth in the recipient is *gratitude.*

I want to highlight the unique part of the definition by Dr. Emonns: "the perception of something as a gift" leads to gratitude. That relates to our outlook on life.

Are we grateful for what we have, or do we feel entitled to it?

I remember visiting my grandmother at Christmastime when I was 8 years old.

While my immediate family opened our presents from each other at home, Grandma's house was where the aunts, uncles, and cousins got together and exchanged gifts.

I received one gift from both my aunt and uncle: a walkie-talkie. It was pretty cool, but I didn't care about that. I was focused on my two cousins of a similar age, opening boxes upon boxes of Christmas presents.

I'm not proud to tell you this, but I threw a fit. I was so upset that my cousins had more gifts to open than I did. What my uncle tried to explain was that my gift was more expensive, and while my cousins had more gifts to open, they cost about the same in total.

Do you think an 8-year-old cared about that? No. They had more than me, and I wasn't OK with that.

While I received a gift, did I perceive it as a gift? Did I react with appreciation and thankfulness? No. I was a spoiled little brat. I felt "entitled" to more, and that entitlement led to "ingratitude."

Ingratitude is the result of comparing what others have with what we don't have. It's a perception of life circumstances that can be a never-ending battle in our consumer culture.

Comparison is one of the great assassins to a grateful heart.

Even if I have a great life, it's not as great as this person over here, so I don't get to be happy. Or at least that's how we might feel at a reactionary level.

Dr. Emmons is telling us that gratitude is a choice. Our capacity to experience gratefulness is in part dependent upon our ability to appreciate what we have.

And if we want to get proactive, we can even start looking for and noticing the gifts that surround us. Those gifts might be a tangible object, they could even be a generous conversation with a friend when you are in a low place.

It's the awareness that, "You didn't have to. But you did. And for that, I am grateful."

# The Pilots

On day three I boarded a flight to Philadelphia for the first-ever Front Row Dads Retreat led by my longtime friend, Jon Vroman.

The Front Row Dads is a community of entrepreneurial fathers who gather twice a year to mastermind about how to become better dads to our kids, and better husbands to our wives, all while running successful businesses. This is a community in which I am very involved, and you'll hear about it a few times in this book.

While I was walking down the tarmac to the plane, I began to think about who would receive my five cards today, and an idea sparked inside my head: the pilots.

During takeoff, I always pray for safe travel, and so far, they've always delivered! Aside from the airlines who own the planes, the pilots are the ones responsible for global air travel.

People fly for all sorts of reasons: vacations, business deals, holidays, funerals, starting life anew. No matter the reason, the pilots take us where we want to go, no questions asked.

I had two legs of this flight, with two pilots on each plane, so that was four pilots to thank before landing in Philly. That would leave me only one card to finish that evening.

While boarding the plane, I asked the flight attendant, "What are the names of the pilots on this plane?"

From the look of confusion and uncertainty she gave me, I realized that she had probably never been asked this question before. And rightly so. Why would anyone need to know the names of the pilots?

Chagrined, I quickly reply, "I'm writing thank you cards to the pilots. That's why I want their names."

She lightened up and said, "Oh, why didn't you say so. Here you go." And she wrote them on a napkin for me: *Jack and Mark.*

I headed to my seat, napkin in hand, and began second-guessing everything I was about to do.

*Am I the first person to write a thank you card to the pilots? They're just doing their jobs anyway, right? Do I really need to tell them thank you? Is this appropriate?*

It was too late to back out. With the flight attendant my new unofficial accountability partner, I had to do it.

> # Suddenly, a mantra came into my head:
> ## "Nothing bad can come from saying thank you."

It's a thank you card, I told myself. If they're going to be weird about it, they're weird.

So, in spite of all my worries, I began to write.

Thus begs the question: How do you thank someone you don't even know?

I imagined myself standing in front of the pilots, looking at them and thinking about their lives. *What must it be like to be you? What do you have to deal with? What do you care about?*

Then it came to me: Nobody becomes a pilot by accident or default. It's not like if you work at Chili's long enough and they eventually make you the store manager. Nobody starts at baggage claim and gets promoted to flying the planes.

You have to want to be a pilot. The standards to which they are held, both mentally and physically, are among the most demanding, and not everyone qualifies for the chance to even try. Those who do qualify train for years for this position. It's probably been a dream of theirs to fly since they were little.

I also realized that one thing that always weighs on me when traveling is that I'm away from my family. But while this separation is a temporary thing for me, for pilots it's everyday life. They probably miss a lot of important family gatherings, holidays, and special events because of their job.

I imagined what it must be like for them to have a severely delayed flight, through no fault of their own, yet still have to fly a plane full of disgruntled passengers who are likely to take it out on them.

In short, they deal with a lot, so I thanked them for it in my letters.

Five hours later, as I walked off the plane, I paused at the open cockpit door and asked, "Which one is Jack and which one is Mark?" They looked at me, confused and a little concerned, but after one of them identified himself, I extended my hand with the cards and said, "These are for you."

One of the pilots accepted the cards and handed the other to his partner. With that, I headed to my connecting flight to do it all over again.

As an aside, the only thank you cards I had on me for this trip were business notecards with my contact info printed on them.

What transpired over the next 24 hours was nothing short of amazing.

Three out of the four pilots personally emailed to thank me for their cards. They commented on how much they love their jobs, but at the same time they mentioned how challenging it is for their families. All in all, they were grateful to receive my notes.

One pilot even told me, "You know John, in my 12 years of flying planes, no one has ever given me a thank you card."

My mind was blown!

I couldn't believe it. For 12 years, this man had been flying tens of thousands of people across the globe and no one had ever taken the time to formally thank him for it. That just didn't seem right.

If that's what it's like for a pilot, I wondered, what must it be like for everyone else?

Thank you for all the hours you spent going through flight school. Thank you for all the time you spent away from your family to help others be closer to theirs.

Thank you for getting up early to fly a bunch of tired grumpy people through the sky.

Thank you for being strong and bold when you have to tell people they are being rerouted to another airport because of weather.

Thank you from all the people on this plane whether they tell you that or not.

Here to serve,

John Israel
Your Grateful Salesman
CutcoJohn@gmail.com

# The Waitress

After landing in Philadelphia, I had a great time on the first evening of the Front Row Dads Retreat. We wrapped up the first session and headed to a small bar to get to know each other better.

As our party of 40+ guys entered the bar, at which we had no reservation, everyone inside stopped what they were doing to turn and look at us. We were a spectacle.

The sour look from the only waitress in the bar read loud and clear, "Y'all just ruined my night."

Her name was Shantae.

Shantae seated us in a back area big enough for our entire party. We ordered drinks, food, more drinks, more food. Slowly but surely, our party dwindled down to 10 of us.

In spite of being short-staffed, Shantae did a terrific job. We could tell she was annoyed at the start, but by the end she had warmed up to us.

She was well-deserving of my fifth and final card for the day.

At 1:30 in the morning, we closed out our tabs, and I wrote Shantae this card:

> *Shantae, Thank you.*
>
> *We are a group of entrepreneurial fathers getting together for a retreat to learn how to become better dads.*
>
> *We know forty+ guys showing up last minute was not how you planned to spend this evening, but you took care of us gracefully. You got everyone's food and drink order correct, which is nearly impossible with a full staff, let alone by yourself.*
>
> *Tonight was all about fellowship and connection, and that's what we got.*
>
> *You could have been annoyed, but you weren't. You could have been rude, and we would have understood. But you were great, and tonight was great ... because you created the space for us to have fun. On behalf of all of the Front Row Dads, thank you.*
>
> *—John*

Shantae was sitting at a far-off table, cashing out her receipts and tips for the evening. I walked up and handed her the card. She looked at me seemingly confused, and I said, "This is for you."

As I walked around the corner and toward the exit, I saw the restroom and realized I should probably pay a visit before our cold walk back to the hotel. I went into the restroom for a moment, and as I walked back into the main area of the bar it was clear that Shantae had read my card. She was standing there waiting for me to come out. Her head was cocked to the side with a big grin on her face.

She ran at me, picked me up, and gave me the biggest bear hug of my life, saying, "That is the best tip I've ever been given."

After she put me back down, we paused for a moment and just looked at each other. For a brief moment, we saw each other not as waitress and customer, but human being and human being. Respect, love, and gratitude permeated the space between us.

I looked at her and said, "You deserved it." Both of our eyes welled up with tears, we hugged once more, and I headed out the door. The entire exchange must have only lasted five seconds, but it's five seconds I will never forget.

As I walked back to the hotel, I told myself, "The world needs this. The world needs us to see and appreciate each other for our greatness, not our weakness. I will … I must finish this mission of writing five thank you cards every day, no matter what it takes.

That was day three.

# Appreciation and Connection

> *"I define connection as the energy that exists between people when they feel seen, heard, and valued; when they can give and receive without judgment; and when they derive sustenance and strength from the relationship."*
>
> —Brené Brown from Gifts of Imperfection

Have you ever heard someone say, "I just don't feel appreciated"? It could be a wife talking about her husband, a husband about his wife. An employee about the boss. A parent about the kids.

But what does it really mean to be appreciated?

The root word for *appreciate* comes from the Latin word appretiare, which literally means *to appraise or set the value of a thing.*

Think of it this way: When people want to sell their home, one thing they must do is get an appraisal of the property. They hire a professional who comes out and whose job it is to inspect every nook and cranny of the home from the window treatments, cracks in the walls, the total square feet, new upgrades, possible pest or termite damage, and a laundry list of other items. Some conditions increase the value, while others bring it down. The sole purpose of this "appraisal" is to assess and <u>assign a value</u> to the property and <u>declare it's worth</u>.

So how does this apply to people? How do we assess the value of another human being?

It feels silly even asking the question because innately we realize that human potential is so vast, it's immeasurable.

However, when we ask the question, "What is the value of this person?" we open an inquiry to a world bigger than ourselves and we set the stage for deep, meaningful, human connection.

Let me explain.

On the day-to-day, most of us are just concerned with ourselves. We wake up and worry about how much sleep we got or didn't get, to which we wonder how that will affect our performance throughout the day. We jump on Facebook and compare our failures with others' successes, or our successes with others' failures. We judge, assess, and assign meaning as it relates to our model of the world. We are the appraiser of our own life.

Here's a visual that might help you understand.

The other day I was driving past a park when I saw children playing soccer. That's not unusual. What's unusual was that they each wore a giant bubble suit, four feet in diameter. It covered from the tops of their heads to their knees, so they had room to run, kick, and bounce off of each other without getting hurt. It was an entertaining sight, to say the least.

It got me thinking: The human experience is kind of like that. It's like we are all running around with these giant transparent bubbles surrounding us. Inside that bubble is our life. Our experiences, our goals, our trials, struggles, what we deal with. It's our life. To us, it is everything and nobody knows it better than we do.

However, to the degree that we hold the significance of our bubble, is the degree to which we stay disconnected from others.

When we ask the question, "What's the value of this other person?" we are forced to step out of our bubble in order to peer in to someone else's so that we can understand them and where they are coming from.

When appreciating a total stranger, sometimes I just give my best guess, oftentimes I just ask them. "How long have you worked here? Why do you do this job? What's hard about it for you? What's your long-term plan?"

During another trip, I had the fortune of sitting next to my pilots during a flight delay. I was able to ask all the questions I wanted to know about being a pilot. Of the two men, one shared that this would be his first year, in 22 years of flying, that he gets to spend Christmas Day with his family.

The more I got to asking those questions, the more empathy I had for them. The more I got to see their model of the world, the more I could appreciate it. They weren't just guys doing a job. They were people just like me out to contribute to the world the best way they knew how.

In contrast with the home appraiser, the more we understand the challenges or problems people face, the higher value their actions hold.

What's more valuable: a pilot, or a pilot who's missing Christmas with his own family, so you can be closer to yours?

What's more valuable: the waitress who gave you excellent service, or the waitress who gave you excellent service despite the fact that you showed up with 40+ of your friends, unannounced, with no reservation, to which you kept her busy until 2 o'clock in the morning?

Who's to say you'd know the difference if you weren't present and curious enough to see it?

That is the big lesson. Curiosity is the precursor to appreciation and appreciation is the birthplace of empathy. With empathy we grow in compassion, and the more compassion we have, the more deep and meaningful ways we connect.

This applies for husbands with their wives, and wives with their husbands. Senior management with their employees, and employees with their senior management. Parents with their kids and kids with their parents, and so on and so on.

When we grow in empathy and compassion, the dividing lines of our roles disappear, and we are just humans connecting with other humans. We all bleed. We all feel. We all show up for a reason.

Now, what is that reason? That's up to you to find out.

## Get Started Today:

Today, pick someone and practice appreciating their world. Ask yourself these questions:

| | |
|---|---|
| What's it like to be them? | What are their struggles? |
| What's great about them? | What do they care about? |
| What's beautiful about them? | Why are they here? |
| What are their challenges? | |

If you feel so called, write the person a note. You might hand it to him. You might leave it for her to find. Regardless of your approach, notice how your demeanor and attitude shift merely by thinking through these questions about someone. If you choose to write a note, journal about what you felt or noticed as you expressed that appreciation. Does it feel different to you when writing it rather than just thinking about it?

# Uber Driver

I met Medhani on a 45-minute drive from San Francisco to the Oakland Airport.

As with the pilots on my plane, I didn't know this man. However, I also didn't know what it's like to be an Uber driver.

I was curious, so I asked him:

What's it like to be an Uber driver? Are most people nice or difficult? Have you had any rude customers?

What's the weirdest thing that's happened in your car? Do you like your job?

How many hours do you work per week?

He answered with a smile and we began a conversation. One thing was for sure, people rarely talked to him. His car was much like an elevator: People came and went. He generally sat in silence as he drove them around.

He had a thick accent I didn't recognize, so I asked where he was from.

That's when it got interesting. He was from Nigeria and had been living away from his family in the U.S. for four years. He sent all his money, other than basic living expenses, back home to his wife and kids in the hope that he could one day arrange to move them here.

As a father who was currently on a business trip away from my family, I was touched. However, I had the luxury of being gone only a matter of days, when it had been over six months since Medhani had seen his family.

Thank you for the ride, my friend.

Medhani,

Thanks for the ride to the Oakland airport today. I know it's your job and I paid for it but you did a great job and gave me the space to sit and think.

The honest truth is that I don't know you and you don't know me. So why the hell should I be writing you a thank you note? Well, I find most people are underappreciated in their work. You probably have had to deal w/ a lot as an Uber driver. Happy people, sad people, someone spilling their coffee all over your car, people not leaving 5 star reviews not because of anything you had control over, I mean it's San Francisco & I bet you've seen it all.

Clearly you are doing this for a bigger purpose: your family. I wish you the best as you work hard to get your wife here to America. It truly is a great country and I admire anyone willing to take advantage of the opportunity to make a better life for themselves or their family no matter where they were born. Thanks again for the ride.
        —John Israel

33

# Hotel Housekeeping

I left a thank you card for the hotel house keeping in my room during a multi-night stay in Austin, TX. As you can see, upon my return, she had left her own response.

Housekeeping is supposed to be invisible. Their job is to remain unseen while at the same time making the presence of their service obvious.

What happens when the "unseen" become seen? Do they take more pride in their job? Do they whistle while they work?

I don't know, but I could visualize the smile on the maid's face as she read my note, and the joy she felt while writing back. It brought human connection to a normally disconnected experience.

I gained a higher level of appreciation to know who it was that cleaned up after me. This in turn influenced me to leave my room a little nicer than usual when I checked out.

# **Apple Man:** Acknowledging Honesty & Good Behavior

My experience with Apple has generally been good, but this particular employee went above and beyond.

I visited the Apple store because my iPhone wasn't holding a charge and my headphones had stopped working. Not only did Apple Man fix my phone, but he also switched my headphones out for free (even though they were no longer under warranty). On top of that, when I asked about new watch bands for my Apple Watch, he directed me to a competitor to get a similar-quality band for a lower price, noting that Apple's specialty is the technology, not the accessories.

Now, an Apple executive or store manager might be frustrated that this employee didn't sell me the headphones or the watch band, but the reality was, Apple Man could tell I was already a huge Apple junkie. He spoke with me like I was a friend who he was looking out for, not just another customer.

Whatever he might have lost with a small purchase was replaced with greater returns on loyalty for years to come.

I dropped this note off for him the next day.

Eight months later I came into the store for a purchase and who do I see? Apple Man. After recognizing each other, he shared that my card meant so much that it's still hanging on his fridge.

Apple man,

Thanks so much for helping me yesterday. You seriously went above and beyond giving me replacement headphones for free when I was trying to buy them, then after buying a new case and asking about apple watch bands, you referred me to Amazon for comparable 3rd party products.

I buy tons of Apple products and that's the reason why you guys hire honest people who just want to help. My mom bought her 1st mac in 95 when I was 12 and have never owned another computer brand since. You guys are great. You were awesome. Just thought you should know!

Here to serve,

John Israel
Your Grateful Salesman

CutcoJohn@gmail.com

# Goodbye, Stuff

I stared into my closet at the sea of clothes I couldn't bear to part with. A box marked "Goodwill" sat next to my feet. It was go time. This would be the day I got rid of all my "stuff."

During the first month of the Mr. Thank You Project, my wife and I decided to move to Dallas, Texas. Well, we actually decided six months prior that we were moving, but today was the day we started packing.

If you've ever moved, you understand what it's like to deal with all the "stuff" you've accumulated throughout your life, or at least since your last move.

As I peered into my closet, a knot formed in my stomach. I didn't want to let any of it go.

My ego said, "I paid good money for that item. I don't want to just give it away. Whoever gets it won't appreciate or value what I know it to be worth."

My rational mind kicked in and said, "Well, there will be a time when I need this thing, and if I throw it away, I'll have to buy a new one."

Suddenly I'm thinking, "Maybe I'll just take it all with me." Then, as I remembered the minimal room that would be left in the moving truck, I realized it was time to part ways with these unneeded garments.

As I listened to my uncomfortability, I asked myself, "Why am I so resistant? I haven't worn most of this stuff for at least two years."

The more I thought about it, the more I realized, these weren't just clothes, they were memories of experiences.

I saw the two suits I had custom-made in Thailand when my best friend Nick and I visited there during the Christmas break of our senior year in college. I saw an old favorite leather jacket that I splurged on when I had a big sales day. I brushed my fingers over the dozen or so collared shirts I used to wear every day when I was a manager, and all the ties that matched.

I thought, "Whoever gets these clothes won't appreciate their value. They won't know what they've been through."

Then a lightbulb went off. "What if the receivers <u>did</u> understand the story behind each item?"

That's when I decided to write a thank you card to go along with my most meaningful articles of clothing.

I thanked the buyer for picking such a "fine garment" from the display. Then I explained the significance of the piece and why it wasn't "just an ordinary suit." I got to share how one particular jacket was a favorite because of its comfortability, regardless if my wife thought it was ugly or not.

I either safety-pinned the note, or shoved it into one of the pockets. I didn't need to write the letters for each piece of clothing, just the most important ones I was afraid to let go of. In fact, once the momentum began, I gave away more than I was planning to give away, more quickly and easily than I ever expected.

It was a transformational experience. I shifted from the "fear of loss" to the "joy of giving" almost immediately.

I imagined the purchaser peering through the racks at the thrift store, and picking up this suit, trying it on and then putting his hands in the pockets only to pull out my note.

I thought, "How would I react if I found such a letter?" I'd be elated, and more eager to buy the item than any other just because I knew where it came from. I'd feel connected to the giver and his experience. Almost like I was absorbing his superpowers or adopting his life experiences. Like I was part of a life-relay, and one day it would be passed on to someone else.

What a different experience than the separation anxiety I felt when I first starting the purging process.

"But why did this work so well?" I asked myself.

It's not in the writing of the thank you card per se, that made the transformation. It was in getting to share the story and its significance that I felt empowered to let everything go.

When some part of us is in pain, it's as though that part desires to speak loudly so that it isn't ignored. But until we acknowledge it, and listen to it, that part will just keep on flaring up and speaking out. By listening to those parts of ourselves, and honoring their messages, the intensity of the pain dissipates.

And if we can find a way to celebrate that experience, we can transform its nature from being one of "significance to avoid the recurrence of pain" to the "reminder of a transformational moment in which we chose to make positive meaning out of a difficult experience."

This isn't expected to be in just a moment's notice. I was just dealing with clothes here. There are a multitude of life experiences that will take more than a thank you card to fix. But it might be a start. Baby steps.

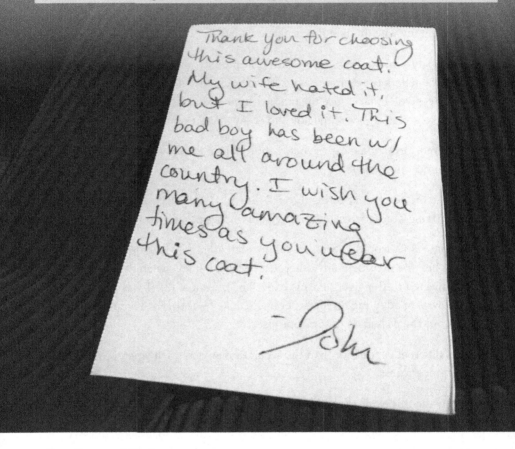

### Get Started Today:

Try it. Take an article of clothing or an item in your house that you adore but never use or wear anymore. Maybe a suit, or a dress, or a lamp. Write down why this item was so special to you, and thank the person who buys it. Then pin, tape, or stash the note somewhere, and give it away.

Notice how you feel, and see if that inspires you to be more generous in what you give away.

# Christmas Lights: Appreciate What You Want to See More Of

Seventy-nine days into my journey, I was feeling a bit stuck. It was December by now, and I had already written 395 thank you cards. I started to worry that I was running out of people to thank. I had written letters to family, friends, clients, and clearly many interesting people I'd met along the way. However, with winter upon us, work had slowed down, and my reserves of people who I could write thank you cards to, was dwindling.

I shared this struggle with a good friend who told me, "John, just appreciate whatever you want to see more of in the world."

His words struck a chord with me. Could it really be that simple?

The next day, I went for a walk with my 2-year-old son, Anderson. While on the walk, Anderson jumped out of his stroller and ran into a neighbor's yard and started pointing and yelling out the colors of the Christmas lights.

It was adorable.

I thought, *Man, I really appreciate people who take this season to heart, those who put forth the energy and effort to decorate their homes. It makes my son smile and in turn, makes me smile. I want more of that!*

With those thoughts in mind, I wrote a simple note to all the homeowners in my neighborhood who decorated for Christmas.

When we appreciate others for doing something that makes us happy, we ignite the desire in their hearts to do it again ... and again ... and again.

Dear neighbor.
Thank you for taking the time and energy to decorate your house for Christmas. We just moved to the neighborhood from California and were delighted to see a handful of people who made the effort. Every day we walk our 2 year old to the playground and he would run over and announce the colors of the lights in your yard. It made him smile and in turn it made us smile. Thank you & Merry Christmas,

- The Israel's
on Odessa Dr.

I just imagined myself as that neighbor, going to the mailbox and reading this note from someone who valued and admired all the efforts I had put into decorating my home.

I then thought about the effort to break all those lights and decorations at the end of the season, boxing them up, and storing them in the garage. Then, 11 months later, when it's time to decorate the home again, I'd probably feel the pain of the effort. "Ughhh … this is going to take forever. Is it really worth it?"

In that moment of "Is it worth it," would I recall the note written by a neighbor? Would I be more willing to push through the effort and energy if I knew it mattered to someone?

While I couldn't speak for my neighbors, I knew how impactful this would be for me.

If you want more good things in your life, appreciate those things you consider as good. If you want more Christmas lights in your neighborhood, appreciate your neighbors who decorate. If you want more love in your life, appreciate those who love you.

Appreciation, for the most part, costs nothing—just a bit of time, some ink, and a little courage.

## Get Started Today:

When you look at your everyday life, what do you want to see more of? What are the simple joys or pleasures that are easy to overlook? Who makes those possible?

If you're in a leadership role at work, think about the people who positively affect your company culture without being asked, and without extra pay. What might it mean to them to have their work acknowledged?

You might consider writing them a note, or simply taking 30 seconds to tell them how much you appreciate it.

What do you notice? How do you feel? How do they react? What changes, or more importantly, what continues to show up?

If you feel called, tell us the story at: **www.MrThankYou.com**, or share about it in the Mr. Thank You Project Facebook community.

# It's Not the Length of the Note That Matters

What I didn't expect was the length of time I'd spend writing thank you cards every day. It took an average of one and a half hours every day to write five cards. A comment I often received was that the notes weren't a simple, "Hey thanks for that thing you did." I wanted each one to be thoughtful.

However, regarding gratitude, it's not the length of the note that matters, as I learned from an experience with my wife.

I love my wife, Monica. She really is an extraordinary woman, so it goes without saying that she received more than three thank you cards during this year-long gratitude journey.

Of all the notes and letters I wrote her, my wife said that the one pictured here was the most meaningful.

Here's the set up. Every morning, I wake up before Monica and make a French press of coffee. I drink half, and pour the other half in a carafe for her to enjoy when she wakes up.

One day during month two of the Mr. Thank You Project, before leaving for work, I realized that we had run out of coffee.

This wasn't a big problem for me because I could stop at Starbucks on the way to meet my first client. However, my wife and I had just moved into our new house with our 2-year-old and 1-month-old boys, and we shared one car. Unless she walked the two miles to the nearest coffee shop, she'd have to go a day without coffee on top of watching our boys all by herself—and this while contending with the consequences of waking up every hour to nurse our newborn son.

I knew this would be an issue, but I was running out of time. In the area where we live, if you miss the "before traffic" window, you can add 30 minutes to an hour to your commute, no matter where you are going.

Monica walked downstairs to kiss me goodbye, and I said with a terrified grin, "Oh, by the way, we're out of coffee."

In a matter of seconds, her half-awake brain put together all the information I just shared with you. A look of despair came over her face. It was about to be a rough day.

I drove off to Starbucks, and as soon as I hit the drive-thru, something didn't feel right.

Just the previous week I had written my wife her first thank you note. It was filled with all the things I loved about her and was grateful for, including her willingness to forgive my mistakes. Would this be another opportunity for her to forgive me or was this an opportunity to make her day?

Sure, it was going to add half an hour to my commute if I drove back home to give her a cup of coffee, but what would that show her? What impact might it have?

I knew what I had to do. I ordered two grande drip coffees to go, drove the 15 minutes back to our house to drop it off, and left this note.

While I hit the traffic barrage that morning, I got to spend those extra 40 minutes happy and proud of myself, rather than spending the entire day feeling bad for my wife knowing what she was going through.

My client wound up being late anyway, so it worked out all around.

# How Do We Treat That for Which We Are Grateful?

When we are grateful for something or someone, we treat them with a different level of respect. We use more care and consideration.

In the natural course of life, when we have more good things happening to us, it would make sense that we would be more grateful. But is that always the case?

I have a close friend named Hal, who wrote the foreword to this book, who was diagnosed with an aggressive form of leukemia. We didn't know if Hal would make it. For an entire year he was in and out of the hospital for chemotherapy.

Fortunately, Hal beat cancer and is in remission.

In talking with Hal after his recovery, I asked him, "What's different now than before you had cancer?"

Hal shared that one of the things he had taken for granted was the relationship with his kids. In the past, Hal would start his mornings early and work from home. His 6-year-old son would often ask him to play, and Hal would push it off until the end of the day when his work was done. By then, Hal was tired and didn't have much energy to give.

Post-cancer, Hal now spends the first 30 minutes of his day playing rather than working. He says his son deserves his best, not his leftovers.

At the heart of gratitude are humility, respect, and an understanding that life is bigger than we are. It's the realization that what is here today may not be here tomorrow, but because it is here in this moment, we will honor it.

> During this year-long gratitude challenge, I was forced to ask myself, **"If I am truly grateful for this person, how should I treat them?"**

It's quite a challenge to commit to express more gratitude in your life, because along with it comes the responsibility to honor the coinciding emotions and side effects.

By side effects, I mean how people begin responding to you.

Early in this journey, I wrote a thank you card to the front desk assistant of my office building, Angela. She doesn't work for me directly, but she greets and directs everyone who comes in, including my clients. In effect, she does impact my business.

I shared with Angela how impactful her warm demeanor is as the first impression clients have when they come in. I also thanked her for always having coffee ready in the common area, and for the wonderful pies she bakes for everyone during the holidays.

After giving her the thank you note, Angela's kind behavior quadrupled. In fact, she became almost too helpful, knocking on my door to tell me about extra food in the kitchen, or just asking if I needed anything before she went home for the day. I started thinking, "I have work to do. Stop bothering me."

I had to check myself. If I am going to say thank you to someone, I don't just get to disappear and go back to life as usual. There is an enhancement in that relationship I am now responsible for.

I warn business and sales people about this. You don't get to tell clients how much you value and appreciate their business and then not return their voicemails or emails. The nature of a business person's claim to be "committed to service" is negated by a lack of follow-through.

Some might say that expressing more thanks and appreciation brings with it more obligation. I like to think of it as opportunity. When gratitude becomes a habit or internal value, you have a new lens to view how to respond to situations and people.

Expressing gratitude begets more gratitude. When you put more out, you get more back—and the more you have, the more you have to give. The only way you can screw it up is to stop giving or stop allowing yourself to receive.

A life filled with gratitude is a life filled with respect for yourself and respect for others. It's a life where you think twice as you make your schedule to consider the other commitments you have made to people who matter to you. Living with gratitude at the center of your life might even change something as seemingly insignificant as the food you order, because if you are grateful for your health, you'll respect your body and what certain foods do to you.

Gratitude is not an easy, soft emotion. It is one that draws forth the best version of yourself that loves you, the life you live, and those around you.

I hope you are ready for it.

# Writing to Non-Humans

Alright reader, are you ready to get a little weird?

"Have you ever written a thank you card to a non-human?" a woman asked me. Her name was Jen.

I had just finished sharing the Mr. Thank You Project at a women's leadership conference in Miami, Florida, and was doing some Q&A over lunch. I was a bit surprised yet intrigued by this particular question.

"What do you mean non-human?" I asked curiously.

Jen continued, "Well, I have this dog I rescued from a shelter. I love my dog. I could think of a dozen or so things that I can appreciate about my dog. Have you ever written a letter to an animal? Does it still fit in the parameters of your project?"

I still wasn't quite sure if she was serious. I responded, "I guess it would count. There's nothing that specifies that the cards must be written to another human. However, since they can't read, you'd probably need to read it to them," I said half-jokingly.

"That's what I was thinking. I can write it, then read it to him out loud." She was dead serious.

When I came home the next day, I couldn't stop thinking about Jen's question. I had always imagined the scope of the Mr. Thank You Project being in relation with other people. However, as I thought more about it, the heart of the project is to elevate one's personal level of gratitude. Another way to look at that would be to increase one's appreciation for the life one lives and everything inside of it.

It got me thinking about our dog Joey.

Joey is a chihuahua-terrier mix. Seven years ago, we adopted him as a puppy from a friend.

We didn't have kids yet, and my wife thought getting a dog would be good "practice" for being parents. While I completely disagreed with this comparison of a child and an animal, she still convinced me to at least "see the dog" before I made my decision.

We went to our friend's house and waited for the dog in the front yard. I can still remember his little sunken puppy dog face as he walked sheepishly over to me, sat directly on my lap and rested his head on my leg. I'm still convinced that my wife and her friend choreographed the whole thing. I couldn't say no.

We drove home with our new dog, and affectionately named him Joey after Joey Tribbiani, a character from one of our favorite TV sitcoms, *Friends*.

Joey grew on me and, with time, he became more my dog than my wife's.

Unfortunately, when we started having kids, he became the house dog, rather than the family dog. We paid less and less attention to Joey. We hardly walked him, we rarely played with him. Joey had just started to blend in with the background of our household.

As I came home from my trip at the women's conference, Joey was at the front door, barking and wagging his tail to greet me, as he always is.

Joey followed me upstairs to my home office where he settled in under my desk. I grabbed a pen and some stationery and told myself, "This is so weird."

I proceeded to write a thank you card to my dog.

I then lay on the ground, looked Joey straight in the eyes and read him his letter.

While I can't speak for Joey, I can tell you about the visceral love, appreciation, and sadness that came out as I read his note.

Joey had always shown up 110 percent to be my buddy and companion, and I had gotten too busy to appreciate or take care of him. That was going to change.

From that moment, we started playing more often, going on regular walks with the kids, and after I kiss the kids goodbye when I leave for work, Joey gets one too. And if I ever forget, my 2-year-old reminds me, "Kiss Joey. Kiss Joey."

It's disgustingly cute, but my relationship with that dog changed.

When we express our love and appreciation for something or someone, it's like we agree to continue to honor, support, and respect them. It's one thing to think it, it's another thing to write it down and declare it verbally.

I can tell you the same for most of the relationships in my life. After expressing gratitude to and for them, things changed. We interacted differently together. We shared more love and mutual respect.

I love my dog. He is a wicked awesome dog, and my renewed sense of appreciation for him made me curious ... where else could I take this challenge to explore my capacity to appreciate?

Dear Joey,
    I am so glad that your original owners returned you so that Monica and I had the opportunity to adopt you. I am literally happier because of you. You are excited to see me when I come home, even when it's been a tough day. No matter how I feel or what mistakes I've made, you always bring me level 10 - love.
    I'm sorry we haven't spent much time w/ you since the boys have been born. You deserve better. I will do my best to give you the level of respect and attention you have given us. You are my protector, you are my homey. Love you bud.
                    - John

47

# The Gratitude Loop: Thank You, You're Welcome

Eight years ago, I had spoken at a sales conference and my topic was on client relationships. After finishing my talk, I stepped down from the stage and exited the conference. A young woman cornered me in the lobby to thank me for my talk.

"This was exactly what I came to this conference to learn," she told me.

I replied, "Yeah, well I missed a couple of big parts that were really important to the whole message. I was running short on time. I'm sorry about that. It could have been better."

With a confounded look on her face, the young woman replied, "Well … I thought it was great." Then she turned and walked away.

Her reaction and quick retreat woke me up from my self-deprecation and I realized I had completely blown off her compliment. Then I thought, "Did I just respond to someone's thank you with an apology? What is wrong with me?"

It's moments like these that other people's reactions to our ridiculous actions can be helpful in correcting our behavior.

I couldn't take a compliment. I was uncomfortable receiving love, gratitude, and appreciation. Even as the Mr. Thank You Project began, I noticed that whenever someone would try to compliment me, I'd get fidgety, uncomfortable, and divert the compliment to some other source.

It was either an effort by someone else on my team that deserved the true acknowledgment, or luck, or chance, or good economic conditions. But never the efforts of one John Israel.

But how do we break this bad habit or pattern?

**One day I came up with this concept of the GRATITUDE LOOP.**

## GRATITUDE LOOP

You're Welcome

Thank you

## OPEN GRATITUDE LOOP

Thank you

The gratitude loop is a way to look at compliments, gratitude, and appreciation in how they connect us with another person. It begins when someone acts generously by giving something of value. It might be a physical gift, a compliment, an acknowledgment (a thank you card, perhaps).

When someone acts generously like this, imagine an invisible loop opening up halfway. The moment we respond to that person who gave the compliment with "thank you" or "you're welcome" (depending on the context of what was given or said) the loop closes up. The experience is complete, both parties have been honored for their efforts and value, and the energy in the relationship lives at a higher level of mutual appreciation. Good-feels all around.

What about the opposite experience?

Imagine you are standing directly opposite someone. You look at the person in the eyes and genuinely, authentically say, "Thank you." Now imagine that person looks back at you and says nothing. No feedback, just silence.

The gratitude loop is left open. How do you feel?

This is a fun exercise I like doing with groups because it brings a lot of awareness to the impact on people when we don't accept a compliment or acknowledgment.

When we debrief, the "giver of thanks" often says, "I felt frustrated. Even angry. I allowed myself to be vulnerable and they gave me nothing back."

It's uncomfortable. It's weird. It almost seems offensive.

Even the "thanks receivers" say they feel awkward. They want to say something.

This is what it looks like when gratitude is expressed in an isolated experiment when both parties are conscious and present in the moment to what's happening.

Unfortunately, that's not how life works.

On day 44 of the Mr. Thank You Project, I was beginning to have some serious doubts as to whether I should keep going.

Out of the 220 thank you cards I had sent, only 20 people had responded to thank me for their cards or even acknowledge that they received it. Clearly it wasn't about the 20 who did, it was about the 200 who said nothing.

I was really conflicted because, in the moment of writing the cards, I felt totally genuine and heartfelt. But the moment I realized 90 percent of the people didn't say anything, I began to wonder, "Is this worth it? Do people even care?"

It became about me.

Shortly after this experience, a few things occurred that changed my attitude.

I was sitting down for coffee with someone in my family that I had sent a card to. This person also had said nothing about the card (not that I was going to bring it up).

During our conversation we began talking about real life and what was going on with each other. This person really vented from the heart about deep struggles she was going through with her significant other.

She finished by saying, "That's why I never responded to your thank you card. I wanted to be grateful for what you said, but I just couldn't. I was in so much pain that I couldn't be present to anything positive in my life."

I was taken aback. In that moment I experienced total and full empathy with this person. We sat there, cried together, and had a great conversation that might help their relationship.

I stopped caring if people replied or responded to my thank you cards from then on, because I had no idea what they were going through or dealing with.

Not to mention, some people had the best intentions to reply, got busy and forgot.

One such experience happened to me when I received a thank you card back from a friend in response to the card I wrote. It was during a very busy week and I meant to message the person to appreciate the kind words, but I forgot.

It didn't mean I didn't care about what the person said, or that I had unresolved beef that I was holding on to (the mental conversations I was having with myself about the people who didn't respond to my cards).

This person texted to ask if I received the note. I simultaneously felt embarrassed, thanked them back, and gave up any need to hear from anyone about my cards.

While gratitude is the emotion we feel when receiving a gift or experiencing something (or someone) as a gift, expressing gratitude is also a gift. It is a gift given freely without needing anything in return.

Here are two glaring lessons from these experience:

**1) ACCEPT COMPLIMENTS AND REFLECT GRATITUDE.** If someone takes the time to give you a gift, pay you a compliment, or acknowledge the great work you do—pause, soak it in, and say "Thank you" or "You're welcome."

There's something to be said for being humble, and there's another thing to be said for allowing others to contribute to your life. It's not as much about glorifying you, as it is honoring the vulnerability and generosity of another person bold enough to take the time to appreciate you.

**2) GIVE UP THE NEED TO BE APPRECIATED FOR YOUR GENEROSITY.** Now this may sound counter-intuitive after explaining the whole gratitude loop. Yes, when people don't reflect back that they received or valued our gifts, compliments, or acknowledgments, the natural reaction is that "something is missing." The loop feels open.

True gratitude is expressed with nothing expected in return. When you feel the frustration that someone didn't appreciate what you did for them, just remember, you never know what other people are going through in their lives. Accept that you did a good thing, pat yourself on the back, and move on.

# The YNK Factor

Around month four, in the midst of writing thank you cards to friends from all over the country, I got a reply from my friend Julian in New Orleans, Louisiana. Julian is a top sales guy, and I've always had tremendous respect for him.

On one occasion he generously allowed my family and me to stay at his house for a week while touring New Orleans. Julian even took a week off work to show us around and teach us about the Creole culture in which he grew up. We ate everything in sight, listened to live jazz music on the street, shared a drink on Bourbon Street, and eventually went with him to the Lower Ninth Ward to see the remaining devastation from Hurricane Katrina. It was an eye-opening and enriching experience.

I had much to appreciate Julian for—not only his willingness to allow an entire family to take over his house for a week, but for his commitment to living life at a level ten.

Whether it was business, or his excitement to become a father (his wife was pregnant at the time), Julian was driven to be his best.

A few weeks after receiving my note, Julian visited our home in Dallas while attending a conference. We graciously opened a room for him and his wife.

Julian told me, "John, your note came at the perfect time. What you probably didn't realize is that I was going through one of the toughest times in my life and feeling really down and out. Your letter changed all that. I cried when I read your note because it reminded of my best self and the good things I'd done with my life. What you said completely changed my attitude and really helped me through that time. It was wonderful to have your family visit New Orleans, and you are welcome anytime."

I had always viewed Julian as an amazing guy, and very successful. It surprised me to hear he was feeling anything less than great.

This reaction became common enough that I began calling it the YNK Factor.

## YNK means *You Never Know.*

You never know what people are going through. You never know whom your kind words or actions will touch. You never know how far the ripple of your decisions will go. Even so, believing that those ripples exist, what would you like them to be?

"Your note came at the perfect time" is a statement I've grown accustomed to hearing.

It blows me away to learn how many people are struggling in silence. For some it's simply a downer of a day, while others have major life issues or decisions to make.

In these moments, hope and encouragement are the greatest gifts one can give.

It's easy to forget about the impact we can have on people. It's easy to lose ourselves in the act of winning and accomplishing or working on what seems urgent.

Let us never forget that all around us people are fighting the good fight, and many are ready to give up. A simple note, a short conversation, a text, or an email could make the difference between giving up and persevering.

We can't control what happens to the seeds we sow, but we can control the fact that we sow seeds at all.

# The Gratitude Wall

As serendipity often works, the moment I released the need to receive credit, or acknowledgment for the thank you cards I had been sending, my own mail box started filling up.

Almost like clockwork, I began receiving approximately three thank you cards every week from people who had received one of my cards or who heard about the journey.

While some letters were merely a few kind words of appreciation, others were all-out, full-page expressions of gratitude.

I kept them in a folder for a short while, but decided to start hanging them on the wall. Now they are an ever-present reminder of the impact this work has had on my community and its increasing reach around the world.

# Thank You for Making Something Great

At the end of our lives, we'll get to look back and ask ourselves, "Did I make a difference?"

While we all have an opportunity to make a difference, even if it's just within our families, some people commit their lives to making a big, global impact.

Authors, government officials, CEOs, and founders of companies out to do good were next on my list.

At first I thought, "These guys probably get letters all the time." Then, after seeing people's reactions to my letters, and hearing how often people said, "No one handwrites letters anymore. We just get emails and text messages," I began to think that maybe a letter might make a better impression.

People often ask, "How did you get everyone's address? Especially high-level executives or influencers?"

Simple. I went to their websites and found their addresses in the contact section. If they didn't have an address listed, I'd send a personal email through their website and simply say, "I wanted to send a thank you card to. What's the best address to send to so they actually get it? :)"

Nine times out of ten, they sent me the address. And while yes, a few celebrities had "fan base" websites that I was directed to, many of these individuals emailed me back personally, or at least their direct personal assistants did.

What blew me away was not just how open or receptive they were, but how many of them reached back out with a typed, hand-signed note, or even a personal email directly from the person.

Here is a list of some of the people and organizations I sent cards to, and the copy of a very special response sent back by one of them.

## Authors:

Beth Moore — Breaking Free

Dan Poynter — Self-Publishing Manual

Matthew Kelly — The Rhythm of Life, and The Seven Levels of Intimacy

Jay Papasan — The ONE Thing, a favorite business book James Malinchak — Success Starts with Attitude

Jon Acuff— Start, Do Over, Finish (see what he did there?)

John Maxwell—The 21 Irrefutable Laws of Leadership (as well as 40+ other titles) Seth Godin — Linchpin, Purple Cow, and other marketing books I love

Steven Pressfield — The War of Art, Do the Work, Turning Pro

## Companies:

Apple

Trader Joe's grocery store The Home Depot Landmark Education

Melissa & Doug toy company Whole Foods

Government Officials and Organizations:

Local City Mayor

The IRS (love them or hate them, they build the roads) Governor

President of the United States

**BARACK OBAMA**

October 6, 2017

Mr. John Israel
Plano, Texas

Dear John:

Thanks for your kind message. Michelle and I have been touched by the words of support we've received from Americans across our country, and I appreciate the time you've taken to write.

I'm proud of the progress we've made together. Thanks to the participation and resolve of everyday Americans like you, our country is a better and stronger place today than it was before I took office. None of our accomplishments were inevitable—they were the result of people from every background and station in life stepping forward and embracing the important responsibilities of citizenship. As long as we continue working in common effort and presuming the inherent goodness in one another, I'm confident our brightest days will always lie ahead.

Again, thank you for writing. It was the honor of my life to serve as your President, and while there are many milestone moments we will always remember, it was my conversations with people like you that kept me going every single day. They've stayed with me, and they always will. Thanks for everything—I wish you the very best.

Sincerely,

# My Roommate from Prison

When I was 23, I was roommates with an ex-con. His name was Tarik. Now, I didn't know this until we had been living together for a few months, but had he never told me, I wouldn't have guessed it.

Tarik was the most honest, transparent, friendly, and self-disciplined person I had ever met. He'd go on to tell me I was meeting Tarik 2.0.

"Tarik on Tour" as he was called in his party days, was a very different person. He dealt and used drugs of all kinds, slept with all sorts of women, and acted invincible. Until he was caught trafficking party drugs.

Tarik shared with me his story of transformation over our course of living together, and I grew in a new respect and appreciation for him and anyone who successfully made a transition out of prison.

According to the National Criminal Justice Association, in a 2005 study of 405,000 people released from prison, 68 percent repeat offended within three years; 77 percent within five years.

Well, Tarik was one of these statistics, and after having been through the prison system, and after just a year and a half of being free, he found himself making the same mistakes that would land him back in front of a judge.

Tarik was hopeless and had nowhere to turn, but he had the support of a family friend who recommended a Christian drug and alcohol rehab program.

The rehab program was called Calvary Ranch, based in San Diego, which was a nice, long 2,700 miles from his home and his problems.

Calvary Ranch is a Christian-based program that focuses on three things: community, self-discipline, and faith. While Tarik did not enter as a Christian, he did leave as one.

Tarik was the best roommate I ever had. He was also one of the most grateful people I'd ever met because he knew the alternatives for his life. He had the taste of his freedom being removed from him. Tarik understood the depths of drug addiction and how it ruined his life and relationships. He got one last chance, and he made it count.

Tarik would still go on visits periodically back to Calvary Ranch to be an example of reformation and what God's love can do.

He has been drug-free for 15 years now, and is the executive pastor of a Reality Church in San Francisco. He is married with two kids.

While of course I sent Tarik a thank you card appreciating our friendship, and for the example he set forth for me with his transformation, he opened my eyes to a world I had never known.

Not everyone makes the transformation that Tarik did. He had plenty of stories about prison that would make anyone understand why more than half the people who leave prison go back. Most of these men and women experienced abuse and assault. They witnessed terrible atrocities that the rest of us can hardly imagine.

It's hard to be grateful when you have experienced severe emotional pain and trauma.

There are programs out there designed to reduce recidivism, though the best programs only reduce it by 5 to 10 percent. That may not seem like much, but when you scale that number out, it affects thousands of ex-convicts and immeasurably more people who do not become victims.

In the midst of my yearlong gratitude project, I stumbled upon a prison ministry called Bridges to Life that rehabilitates criminals with violent pasts.

Offenders go through a six-month course where they learn how to deal with the life experiences that led to them making the decisions they did. Also, this program brings in victims of violent crimes, so the inmates can apologize to them and also become aware of the true impact that they have had on others.

John Sage started this program after the murder of his sister. Rather than hold on to his anger, he forgave the criminals and eventually created the program to support and heal both inmates and victims.

I felt the true sense of love that this organization was about and decided to support it and participate in it. I was given a list of recent graduates of their program, and I sent letters of appreciation, encouragement, and congratulations on their accomplishments.

As I wrote every letter, I imagined myself writing to my friend Tarik.

While I realized that, on average, more than 50 percent of people I was writing to would reoffend in some way, shape, or form, I also knew that some of them wouldn't. And some of those men would be examples of complete reformation and they would inspire and support those who have made similar mistakes.

We've all been dealt different hands in life, and we are most commonly the products of our environments and the decisions we make inside of those environments. The reality is, most of these prisoners had experienced more pain and suffering than you or I ever will, and they acted in whatever way that made sense to them.

Many of them feel ashamed, unloved, and unforgivable for what they have done (as do a lot of people NOT in prison, by the way).

We can judge, or we can appreciate progress.

As Tarik would tell me, he's still an ex-con and every day he's one bad decision away from heading down that destructive path. But knowing he has the support, and knowing he has people who believe in him, makes all the difference.

# Blessing Bags

While living in Santa Barbara in my early 20s, I befriended a young guy named Josh. What was special about Josh was that he had a real heart for the homeless.

Anyone who asked Josh for money would get more than a quarter in the coffee cup. They'd get a full-on conversation.

Josh would ask questions, listen to their life stories, and eventually he'd help them with resources, opportunities, places to go, people to see, and finally he'd pray for them.

At first it was annoying, especially if we were trying to walk somewhere downtown where the homeless population is dense. But you just had to realize, this was part of Josh's identity. It was his gift to be compassionate with the needy.

I remember one time, Josh spent 48 hours as a homeless person just to learn what it was like to live with nothing. He slept on the streets, panhandled for money, experienced the fear of someone trying to rob him, and the general disrespect people had for homeless people.

Josh was only 19 years old at the time.

While I don't think I'd take anything to the extreme that Josh did, it did help me grow in my respect and understanding of homeless people. Yes, some of them are on drugs and generally make poor decisions with their lives, while many of them suffer from mental illness and don't have the support to get the care they need. Some of them genuinely had a bad turn of luck and were forced to live on the streets.

What Josh helped me realize is that circumstances aside, mental health aside—there is nothing different between us.

I wanted to find a way to involve the Mr. Thank You Project, and one day that opportunity came up. Our church was creating what they called blessing bags. A blessing bag is a freezer bag filled with necessities that homeless people need but don't usually ask for. Socks, underwear, soap, deodorant, protein bars, and a bottle of water.

I thought this would be a perfect opportunity to include a note inside the bag so that not only did they get the physical things they needed, but they also get the other things we need for survival: encouragement, hope, and love.

# The **Most** Grateful Man in America

I set Google Alerts for my name. Don't judge.

Whenever my name is mentioned somewhere online, Google sends me an email notification. Funny enough, I get more notifications about when "Elton John visits Israel" than when I actually do something significant.

Today was different.

Two months in to the Mr. Thank You Project, I was asked to speak at a conference for entrepreneurs in San Francisco. While I was just on a panel with two other guest speakers, the audience seemed to really resonate with what I was up to.

Shortly after the event, I noticed several thank you cards starting to show up from the attendees who felt strongly that they needed to pause and appreciate more of what they have and the people who support them. A few even mentioned how they had started their own practice of writing one thank you card every day since the conference.

A few weeks after the event, an email popped in from the executive editor of a major online blog who heard from a friend of a friend that "there's this guy doing this crazy project with thank you cards you should talk to." The blog she worked for was called PopSugar.

Sorry to say, I had never heard of PopSugar as their marketing and content is primarily directed toward women, but with a quick online search, I could easily see that their Facebook page alone had a few million followers.

I agreed to the interview, which would be published for their "New Year's Resolution" series at the start of the year.

We were only a few months into the project at this point, and I had no website, no content, no way for anyone to connect with the mission and participate. I didn't think I'd need to start any of that stuff until the end of the project, but we needed something, stat. I created a simple WordPress blog where I started documenting the journey, which would allow people to follow along or communicate if they had any questions.

In the end, the article was a huge hit. Hundreds of people from all over the world shared the article with their communities. That's not the crazy part.

A few weeks later a news correspondent from ABC News reached out to do their own online story about my gratitude project. Then Fox News Phoenix wanted to have me live on the air. Suddenly I was getting radio stations, podcasters, and bloggers emailing and calling me for interviews.

This is when my "Google Alerts" went crazy.

One such article dubbed me as, "America's Most Grateful Man." While I don't know the accuracy of such a statement (nor how you could actually measure it), I'm sure it made my mom proud.

# The Identity of Mr. Thank You Is Born

Amidst the online publicity that started showing up, a mysterious package showed up at my front doorstep. It was addressed to "Mr. Thank You."

Now at this point in the project, I had not used the name, tagline, or title of Mr. Thank You. Everything was under the original name of the project, "The Year of Thank You."

However, something stuck out to me about the name Mr. Thank You. It represented a new identity.

I was still just a normal guy trying to bring purpose to his work. Thank you cards were not a new idea. Gratitude has been around since the first moment a caveman could sit down to appreciate a beautiful sunset.

What struck me about the name was that Mr. Thank You, or Miss Thank You, or Señorita Gracias, could be an identity, not just for me, but for everyone who takes on their own gratitude journey.

Countless times as people would hear my story, they'd follow up with, "I should do something like that. I have a lot of people I take for granted in my life that deserve to hear thank you from me."

The answer isn't just to start writing thank you cards. It is about being able to express that from which you believe deep inside. It's not an act, but a way of being. And when the idea is brought to the foreground, everyone has that desire to appreciate and love those around them.

While I didn't quite know how or what it would look like, I knew we were on to something that was making the impact of global gratitude that we aimed to create. With all this recent publicity, it was time to start thinking bigger.

P.S. Are you still wondering what was in the package? As you might imagine, inside was a big box of thank you cards, and a message of encouragement to keep doing what I was doing. I still don't know who to thank for it. So, whoever you really are, Mr. Thank You Clause, thank you for the inspiration and the awesome name.

# EMOTIONAL INTELLIGENCE AND GRATITUDE

If your emotional abilities aren't in hand, if you don't have self-awareness, if you are not able to manage your distressing emotions, if you can't have empathy and have effective relationships, then no matter how smart you are, you are not going to get very far.

–Daniel Goldman *Author of Emotional Intelligence*

# Hyper-Emotional Awareness

Being focused on gratitude as a daily practice has made me hyper-aware of my emotional state.

Let me paint you a picture.

One day I came home from a long day of client meetings that did not go well. Every appointment either cancelled, rescheduled, or didn't move toward an opportunity to do business together. It was a rough day that ended in bumper-to-bumper traffic on the way home.

I came home early to work on my thank you cards so that I could have a relaxing dinner with the family.

However, when I unlocked the front door of our home, the dog barked, which woke up our oldest son from his nap. He started crying which in turn frightened our youngest son who had almost fallen asleep in my wife's arms.

Now we had a barking dog, two crying children, and my wife giving me the death stare.

After helping settle the kids down, I walked upstairs to my office, dog in tow, to sit down and write my cards.

Sounds like the perfect setting in which to be grateful, right?

Here was the big question: Can we sit down in a negative or upset state and write thank you cards? Technically, yes—but if we want the cards to be meaningful, no.

So what's the solution? Write inauthentic thank you cards, or try to shift my emotional state to one that empowers me?

This particular day, I sat at my desk for five minutes with a card underneath my pen, but I couldn't find the words. I was still angry and upset from the day's outcomes.

So, I stepped back from my desk, turned off the lights, lay on the floor, closed my eyes, and processed the day.

I allowed every emotion to come to the surface without judgment, and I allowed for every fear or consideration to be felt and released. I lay entirely still and just permitted myself to be with it all.

Think of a snow globe. You know those little glass orbs that you find in a gift shop and when you shake them up the fake snow inside swirls around. Our minds are like the globe and our emotions are the snow.

When we have a highly charged, negative emotional event, it's like we pick up that snow globe and shake it vigorously. In these times it's difficult to see anything past the swirling snow of our emotions.

Trying to be productive, engaged, or grateful when we are upset is really hard. The more we try to stop the snow, the more we keep swirling it around. However, once we set the globe down, the snow starts to slowly, calmly, fall to the ground all by itself. In this place we can see and think clearly.

Our brains respond emotionally before we have the chance to respond rationally. We feel, then we think. Having been human for long enough, we've all said things in the heat of the moment that we regret minutes later. By giving us the time to allow the emotions to settle, we make better decisions.

So that's what I did. I lay on the floor for 10 minutes, processed the day, stood up, and wrote a few notes in my journal about how I was feeling. And then I wrote my thank you cards in a matter of minutes.

It was remarkable.

Writing five thank you cards every day became great accountability for me because it constantly forced me to be present in the moment and ask myself, "How am I feeling right now?"

While it was challenging to carve out the time to write my five cards every day, it was also a terrific opportunity to learn new emotional management strategies to shift myself into a state where I could see the things and people to be grateful for in my life.

It really is a skill and a muscle to build. The more you do it, the easier it becomes.

# Heal Yourself and Heal the World

When the wind broke my tent poles, and freezing rain started flooding in around me, I knew I was in trouble.

At month six of the Mr. Thank You Project, 30 entrepreneurs and I attended a meditation retreat hosted by Epic Impact, the coaching and consulting organization of which I was a client.

What was unique about this event is that we'd spend 48 hours completely alone in the desert surrounding Zion National Park in southern Utah. We were equipped with three guides to make sure everyone was safe, and the meditation teacher leading us was Dr. Michael Brabant from Berkeley, California.

What was surprising about Dr. Michael is that he was my age; 33 at the time. He had spent the last 10 years of his life studying, practicing, and leading meditation experiences. While he was young in age, he had the wisdom of an old sage.

When talking with him, Dr. Michael had ultimate presence. There could be a school marching band in the background and he wouldn't break eye contact from your conversation. He was the real deal and I was excited to learn from him.

I also looked forward to this retreat because, being a parent with two kids at home, I could use a little silence. However, as I'd soon learn, this trip would be far from any vacation.

Our guides gave us the instructions. We would all have separate campsites far enough that we couldn't see each other, but if someone screamed for help, we could hear them. We would all have tents, sleeping bags, warm clothes, and water. We'd give up our phones and watches so that we wouldn't be distracted by the time or whatever was happening in the outside world. We'd also be fasting during this time, which meant we were given only two packs of protein powder to sustain us for two days.

Now you might be wondering: *Why would I go through all this just to meditate?*

The intention was to remove as many of the temptations and distractions of life as possible, so that we would only be left with ourselves. From this place we'd be able to enter a deeper state of meditation.

For years I had heard of several well-known thinkers talk about the importance of meditation: Oprah Winfrey, Steve Jobs, Jerry Seinfeld, and numerous other successful people who had made it a daily practice. Being new to meditation, I wanted a real immersive experience.

Now, being halfway through the Mr. Thank You Project, I was starting to see the potential to create a powerful ripple around the world, but I didn't quite know how or what it would look like. I thought this retreat might give me the clarity I needed to continue to expand the journey.

Just before hiking out into the desert, the guides gave us practical advice ranging from preserving the nature around us, to how to handle an approaching mountain lion.

Wait, what? Let's all get into a calm meditative state, oh and keep your eye out for anything that might try and eat you. My excitement started dissolving into nervousness.

After the guides scared the living daylights out of us, Dr. Michael gave us instructions on what to be pondering for the next 48 hours.

He gave us one question to think about while in isolation:

# Why were you put on this earth?

"Why were you put on this earth? Isn't that the question of all questions that mankind has been asking themselves since the dawn of time? Are we really going to discover that in two days?" I thought, skeptically, to myself.

Dr. Michael followed up with, "Be open to how that message shows up. It might be glaringly big, or it might be strikingly subtle. First we must quiet the mind for the answers to show up."

"Sure, no problem," I thought to myself. "I'll just quiet my mind while I ponder my purpose on earth and keep an eye out for man-eating predators."

Just before hiking out into the desert, Dr. Michael gave us one last piece of advice. He said, "Anything that happens in these next 48 hours was meant to happen."

We hiked out and set up our tents at dusk. While it was warm during the day, the temperature that night hit near-freezing levels. Unable to relax, I slept only a few hours.

The next morning, while devouring one of my two protein powder drinks, I sat on a nearby rock and started to take in the beauty of the nature surrounding me. Zion National Park is a breathtaking site. While it is technically a desert, there are plenty of trees, shrubs, mountains, and hills in the landscape. The environment was completely silent with the exception of birds chirping and bugs buzzing around. Not a car to be heard, not a person in sight. My fears and concerns started being replaced with presence and calmness. I decided to shut my eyes and begin my meditation.

As I sat there in complete silence for about 15 minutes, I felt a drop of water hit my face. I opened my eyes and noticed some clouds forming in the sky. They did not look inviting.

I entered my tent for protection, and within a few short hours, those clouds brought with them freezing rain and stormy winds that snapped my tent poles and nearly wiped out everyone's campsites.

The guides rushed out to tell us that there was a snowstorm coming and that we needed to pack as quickly as possible and hike back to base camp.

Trying to repack a tent into its perfectly compact little bag can be frustrating in the first place, let alone with frozen fingers. Peaceful this was not.

We loaded into a van at base camp where we remained in silence until the facilitators could find a location to house us for the next two days.

With all this going on, we were encouraged to stay quiet, as we were still technically on a 'silent retreat.'

Fortunately, one of the participants owned a local business an hour away that was closed for the weekend. We arrived at his office by nightfall, and slept on the floor like sardines lined up in a row.

I began to feel disappointment rushing through my body. Events like these usually inspire some major breakthrough in me, but I was too cold, hungry, and sleep-deprived to focus.

"What did I get myself into?" I thought.

Then I remembered Dr. Michael's remarks, "Whatever happens was meant to happen." I pushed my frustration aside, and committed to giving my best for the rest of the retreat.

The next morning, with 12 hours left, we went through several guided meditations together.

While sitting in a chair, back straight, feet planted on the floor, hands open resting on my knees, I managed to calm myself down.

It was quiet and peaceful. In my mind, it was like I was sitting in a dark room all by myself and it was completely silent. Until I heard a voice. Not a voice from the outside, but a little voice from inside my head.

It said very calmly and subtly, "Heal yourself." Then a few short moments later it said, "Heal the world."

"Heal yourself, heal the world?" I thought. "What does that mean?"

We finished the retreat later that day, and I couldn't stop thinking about what I heard.

"Where did this voice come from? What does it mean? Heal yourself! I'm just writing thank you cards."

Uncertain, I shared my experience with Dr. Michael.

Like a Jedi Master, he listened deeply to everything I said, paused for a few seconds and then calmly responded:

> "We must first heal the pain in our lives in order to create the space for gratitude to show up. **Before we give that gift to others, we must give it to ourselves.**"

It was like a real-life Yoda was in front of me dropping truth bombs, and I was the immature Luke Skywalker, inexperienced yet curious why I was chosen for this message and this mission.

The whole trip home, I thought about Dr. Michael's feedback. While I didn't quite know what it would look like, I knew his words and this message I received would unfold the next layer of my project.

# Peace Cards

After coming home from the meditation retreat, I was eager to re-engage my life, business, and thank you card project.

While visiting with my work friend Jeremy, he was asking about how I've incorporated the Mr. Thank You Project with my "Gold Group."

The "Gold Group" is a term we used to define the best of our best clients. The ones we've done business with for years, and who we have the potential to continue doing more business with over the years to come.

I realized in that moment that, while I had been writing a card to every new client I picked up, I had neglected to appreciate my favorite clients from the past. In my database, I have about 190 such individuals who are in my Gold Group. That's where I decided to start.

Day after day for weeks, I went through this list and wrote cards to my favorite customers. While it was amazing to appreciate the people who had the greatest impact on my career and, ultimately, my life and family, what was so great were the new conversations that started showing up as many of these clients reached back out to thank me for the heartfelt card they received, and some conversations even turned into more business. I'll discuss this in more detail in the chapter titled The ROI of Gratitude.

What I want to highlight here was the surprising experience that occurred when I saw a specific client's name I had nearly forgotten about.

Her name was Jennifer. Jennifer was a great client and champion of my continued success for years. We became close friends. She knew my wife and kids and always told her business associates they needed to buy from me. It was a great, working relationship.

One day, shortly after she had placed an order with me, something went wrong. Without going through the details, there was a mistake made by both parties. Jennifer sent the incorrect information to engrave on her gifts, but we caught the error and made the adjustments without her knowing about it.

In the world of gifting, timing is everything. It's OK to be early, but never late. While we did the right thing, we also forgot to inform Jennifer of the correction on her gifts and that her order would now be delayed by one week.

Unfortunately, the delivery time for this order was of the utmost importance to Jennifer.

On the expected delivery date, Jennifer texted me, upset that her gifts had not arrived, leaving her empty-handed. I tried to explain how we had corrected her engraving mistake, but she wouldn't have any of it. As a result, Jennifer decided to cancel the order. On top of that, she stopped returning my phone calls or emails.

It was painful. I was angry and frustrated because I believed we were in the right. We caught an error she made, and in fact we saved her money by not sending the gifts with the wrong engraving on them.

Everyone I shared the story with said, "Well, she was being unreasonable. You did the right thing." My justification for being right grew and grew the more and more I shared the story.

Almost one year later, as I sat there looking at Jennifer's name on my "Gold Group" list, I felt those same negative emotions resurface just as they had during our last conversation.

Then I stopped and thought, "Why am I feeling this way? This happened months ago. I should be over this." But I wasn't. My ego still wanted to be right. I wanted her to apologize.

As soon as I recognized the pain that was still present in this relationship, I thought back to what Dr. Michael said. "We must first heal the pain in our lives in order to create the space for gratitude to show up."

In this moment I began to see the dots connecting back to my original mission of the Mr. Thank You Project, which was:

> To explore my capacity to experience and express gratitude. Another way to look at this is: **Where do I not want to be grateful and how can I bring appreciation to that area or relationship?**

I also recalled back to that original definition of appreciate, which is "to appraise" and to consider something from all angles before making a judgment.

As I replayed the scenario that caused the issue, I realized a huge glaring mistake I had made. I broke trust by not being in communication with the delay of Jennifer's order. We knew information she didn't, and it wouldn't have been hard to just call or text her about the delay.

And if I'm being even more honest, I didn't want to tell her about the delay because I thought if she knew of the delay, she might cancel her order. Which is silly because that's what happened anyway and even worse, we haven't done any business since. In reality, I wasn't looking out for her best interest as a client or as a friend.

Wow. When I put all those pieces together, I felt the desires of my ego start melting away. What I was left with was sadness. I missed my friend Jennifer. Business aside, I thought she was a great person and I valued our relationship. I knew I had to make things right.

While I didn't know what I would say, I did realize that a thank you card would not have been appropriate, and in fact could have the opposite effect with Jennifer.

Later that day, I walked through Paper Source, a stationery store near my house, for ideas. Not seeing any cards that fit the situation, I came upon a bin of rubber stamps. At the top, like it was waiting for me, I saw a stamp with a peace symbol.

"Perfect!" I said to myself. "That's exactly what I'm looking for."

I purchased some blank stationery, and stamped this peace sign right on the front of Jennifer's card.

While I didn't know what would come of it, I wrote Jennifer this note:

> *Jennifer,*
>
> *Several months ago, we were handling an order for you and were unable to honor the delivery date you were expecting. Please forgive me. We didn't communicate what we needed and that put you in a tough spot at the last minute. I consider you such a good client and friend that it pains me we haven't spoken since. I am not reaching out to ask for your business, but merely to ask for your forgiveness. I have tremendous respect for you as a business person and mom; I am grateful to have met you and gotten to know you better over the years. I wish you the best in business and life this year ahead. If there's anything I can do for you, please let me know. Take care Jennifer.*
>
> *Sincerely,*
>
> *John Israel Your Gift Guy*

The moment I signed my name at the end of her card, something happened. I felt free. It was like a heavy weight had lifted from my body, and I could breathe deeply again. It's not that I thought about Jennifer every day, but when I did, those bottled-up emotions of shame and anger would surface. Now, all I could think about was how much I appreciated my friend and how much I missed her.

Five days later, I received a text from Jennifer thanking me for the card and acknowledging that the aforementioned issue was "water under the bridge."

She went on to share how much she valued our friendship as well and was happy to reconnect. The next day she even reached out with a product question.

Wait a minute. What just happened? We went from no relationship, cut off communication, to right back to where we were as friends like nothing had happened. How is that possible?

Did I say something magical to manipulate her into changing her attitude? No, I just acknowledged and accepted that for which I was responsible, and shared my authentic desire for friendship above all else. Because in the end, that's what I wanted, and that's what I missed most.

However, the transformation didn't occur when she accepted my apology. The transformation occurred when I realized the relationship was more important than my need to be right, and I took action to be consistent with that belief.

Even if Jennifer had never reached back out and acknowledged my apology, I felt complete.

I realized you can't control how others react, you can only control how you act.

If I had just waited around for Jennifer to call, who knows if this would have ever happened. Not to fault her, because it's not about fault. It's about responsibility.

That's when I learned one of the most valuable lessons of the Mr. Thank You Project.

Whoever takes the most responsibility in a relationship **has the power to change that relationship.**

After Jennifer's experience, I decided to make a list of Peace cards to send out.

This would become by far the most difficult, yet life-altering experiences of my year-long project.

# Thank You — I'm Sorry

Over the next several weeks, after the experience with Jennifer, I wrote approximately 11 peace cards. Some of those people I hadn't spoken to in 10+ years, while others, a matter of weeks. Some people were as close as family (some actually family), while others were people I only had a short, one-time interaction with.

How did I decide who to send these cards to?

Many of my peace cards went to people whom I had cut out of my life for one reason or another. Some of them because of a business deal that went south. Others because of something they did or said, or I did or said, that gave neither party reason to talk to each other.

One such friend was someone whom I kept trying to write a peace card to, but for some reason it felt inauthentic. So I rewrote the card. Then I rewrote it again, and again, and again. It wasn't until the fifth attempt at writing his card that I realized *I just need to call him.*

He answered the phone, we caught up for two minutes, then I said, "Hey whatever happened with (XYZ problem)?" He gave me a really simple answer that totally made sense and I realized that there was no reason to be upset anymore. I replied, "Wow, thanks for explaining that to me. It had been on my mind for months."

He replied, "Thanks for calling to ask and letting me explain." Then we went on to have a terrific hour-long conversation about our lives, businesses, and growing families.

While I didn't count these phone calls as part of my five cards per day, they were extremely relevant to the essence of the project: *exploring my capacity to experience and express gratitude.* Which at this point became: *exploring the areas of life or relationships I am not grateful for and bringing healing to them.*

Sometimes a card is the right tool, sometimes it's not—especially with the peace cards. I couldn't find some people's addresses, and based on how things ended, it might have been odd for me to ask for it. In those scenarios, I would just send a private message on Facebook or an email.

While I received a variety of responses, the most surprising, yet common reaction to my honest heartfelt apologies was: thank you.

Wow. The response to "I'm sorry" is gratitude.

In most relationship breakdowns, it's a two-way street. It's not always completely one person's fault.

Some people responded with their own apology by saying, "Thank you. I'm so glad you reached out. I've felt terrible since (XYZ problem). But I'm the one who should apologize because …"

Often our own vulnerability in these situations allows others to feel permission to be vulnerable themselves and say what they've been wanting to say.

However, a word of caution. DO NOT use an apology in order to elicit an apology. If there is a motive other than to authentically express remorse, people can tell.

Delivering an apology wrapped in "but it's still your fault" or "now it's your turn to apologize" does not work and, in fact, can even have the opposite effect.

On the other hand, when an apology is genuine and real, the most common reaction is, "Thank you."

But why?

The Aramaic word for forgive, "shbag," literally means to "untie." This is a fascinating visual. Imagine when someone wrongs us, or we wrong someone else, that we are suddenly "tied" to this other person through this experience. Picture an imaginary rope attaching you to this other person at the wrists.

When we apologize, and/or the other person forgives us, imagine that rope being untied. Like a prisoner being let go, the reaction to this new freedom is thank you.

It's not as natural to just forgive people for something when they don't directly apologize. In most cases, the "I'm sorry" prompts the "I forgive you."

But do we need an apology to forgive, and do we need to be forgiven for our apology to matter?

Several years ago, I met a man named Max. He was a World War II Holocaust survivor.

Max was a young boy during the war and he lost a majority of his family in the concentration camps. Max, of all people, had every reason to be angry and resentful. However, Max was one of the most peaceful and serene individuals I'd ever met.

After he shared with me his story of surviving as a young boy in Germany, I asked, "How can you be so calm as you share this story? I'd be furious if I were you."

Max responded by saying, "I was angry for a long time. I was a very angry young man. Until one day I had an epiphany. I realized that my anger for them was just like their anger for me. I wanted to kill them all. This had me realize, I am just like them and they are just like me. Had I grown up as they had, in the homes they grew up in, and heard the propaganda they heard, I'd probably have been one of them. The moment I realized all those things, my heart softened and I knew what to do. I forgave them. That is when my anger went away."

Max had shared with me the most extreme form of compassion I'd ever witnessed. While he was never directly able to forgive the soldiers who harmed his family, he was able to forgive them in his heart and in his mind. The moment he chose to forgive the Nazis, the rope that had bound him as a victim was removed.

I believe that is why the most common reaction to an authentic apology is "Thank you," because when someone apologizes, the person is giving us an opportunity to forgive.

"Thank you for your humbleness and willingness to apologize and for creating the space for me to forgive you."

While we don't get to choose if someone apologizes or forgives, we get to choose what we do. And as such, we get to unbind ourselves from being the victim or perpetrator in any given life experience if we are willing to forgive others and especially, forgive ourselves.

By the way, not every peace card that I wrote was met with open arms and empathetic forgiveness.

You may try apologizing to someone, and they turn around and tell you off, or you might own a mistake that gets you fired from your job. These are possibilities.

While I didn't experience anyone yelling at me, nor did I lose my job, I did have a few people who never responded or replied to my letters or messages.

Honestly, it made me sad. Not that I needed them to say anything, but I really hoped that at least they had the opportunity to read what I said and feel my remorse for the mistakes that I made. Maybe they didn't get it. Or maybe it really wasn't as big of a deal to them as it was to me, so they didn't feel the need to respond. Or maybe they forgave me long ago and didn't feel the need to tell me. Or maybe they weren't ready to forgive me. I don't know.

We have to be ready before we can forgive or ask for forgiveness. It's not something that we can force.

I can get that. Whatever way they chose to be, I accepted it. When I was able to accept it, I was able to move forward.

What changed as a result of writing peace cards?

Many relationships rekindled or got better. People respected the courage it took to own a mistake or engage in a problem so that we could both move forward powerfully.

It motivated people to start writing peace cards to people in their lives that they needed to make amends with. This inspired me because I could now see the connection of that voice I heard in my meditation, "Heal yourself, heal the world." Not that I had invented something new. Apologies and forgiveness have been around forever.

I had just taken action with an idea that began to slowly remove the charge from negative events in my life, and it was simple enough (I didn't say easy) that others could follow suit.

I felt more courageous, more willing to love openly, more happy with myself.

With each peace card that I wrote or conversation that resulted, it was as though a layer of my ego was being stripped away. I used to be so stuck on being right all the time, but that became less important. Relationships mattered so much more.

It was like I had a new muscle to flex and it became easier to apologize and forgive and move forward.

While I was amazed at the breakthroughs and the lessons I was learning, I had no idea how much deeper we could take it.

# Changing the Story

When people start a new business, they never imagine the day they shut it down.

In May of 2010, I transitioned from sales to management for the company I worked for. I opened up a district office, essentially like a franchise, and was responsible for the recruiting and training of salespeople in the central coast of California. It only took me four years of this to figure out that I was a much better salesperson than a manager.

That business was like my first child, but what took precedence was the impending birth of my <u>actual</u> first child.

Thanksgiving Day 2013, my wife, Monica, shared the news that she was pregnant. While I wanted to be excited, I was also terrified. Not about being a father, but about the father I was afraid I might become.

I was working 70-80 hours/week and missed virtually all family functions and events. I didn't have a social life, and I had the time to spend with my wife mostly because she worked for me.

It wasn't the making of the life I pictured when first opening the business. Not to fault the business, I just had a problem delegating tasks and wanted to do everything myself. A common death sentence for entrepreneurs.

We weighed the costs and benefits of running the business and ultimately chose to close down operations in January of 2014.

If you've never done it, closing a business is nothing like quitting a job. When you quit a job, you just don't have to show up the next day. When you close a business, there is still a laundry list of responsibilities to handle, such as selling office furniture and equipment, closing out accounts, paying bills, and negotiating out of an office lease.

This took months to complete and wore me down even further.

The worst part was telling everyone who worked for me that they no longer had jobs. Some of these people had been with me since we opened our doors four years prior, and others had started only a few short weeks before. While some individuals would be able to transfer to another location an hour and a half south, it was the end of the road for many of them.

Most people moved on just fine, except me. I was stuck. I felt like I had failed everyone, most especially myself.

I had invested heavily into this business physically, financially, and emotionally. I wanted to curl up into a little ball and hide in a corner. Which is basically what I did for the next two months of my life. With our son's impending birth, I knew that couldn't last.

Fortunately, I was able to make a lateral move inside of the company and start working in our business-to-business gift sales division, which is about where this book began.

Going from sales, to business owner, <u>back</u> in to sales felt like a giant step backward. I became resentful. I wanted to blame everything and everyone else for the business failure, except myself. Instead of taking responsibility, learning from my mistakes and moving on, I'd rather share my sob story with anyone who'd listen and gain agreement that, "It wasn't my fault." This went on for a few years.

Six months into the Mr. Thank You Project, I was venting to my wife, Monica, about a particularly negative experience from closing that business. She interrupted me and said, "Listen. You need to get over this. It's been two years. You didn't fail. Our life is great. We wouldn't be where we are today if it wasn't for that experience. You did a lot of good for a lot of people and you've grown tremendously. Why can't you see that?"

She was right. I was still judging myself for this past failure. Whether real or imagined, I had a story I kept telling myself: The business was a failure.

I knew she was right, but I didn't know what to do about it. Then I thought, "How can I bring gratitude to this experience?"

As I pondered that question and began reflecting on those four years the business was open, I started thinking about all of the people involved who supported it and were a part of the journey. I decided they would be the next recipients of my thank you cards.

It took a whole host of people to make that business run and, for two weeks, I wrote card after card to our old staff, salespeople, vendors, partners, even building neighbors.

I simply thought about each person as an individual and what I appreciated about each of them. I brought up my favorite memories of them and recounted the funny stories we used to laugh about. I also acknowledged them for how much I loved seeing them grow while working together. For the handful who stayed in touch, I expressed how great it was to see their ongoing success.

With each card I wrote, my perspective about the whole apparent "failed business" began to shift. Merely forcing myself to recall my favorite stories and experiences started to change my awareness that, "It wasn't all that bad." And as soon as I began expressing those stories, and sharing them with everyone who was involved, it began to change my heart and ultimately my belief about that time in my life.

After sending these cards, the emails, phone calls, and Facebook messages started rolling in from everyone. People reflected back to me how grateful they were for that time in their lives, and how great it was to work with me, next to me, or for me.

One card in particular made its way to the parents of one of my first staff members. He didn't live there anymore, but his mom would phone him to go over any mail that showed up for him.

His mom opened the note and read it out loud to him. Later, he sent me a private message on Facebook sharing how much it meant for his mom to hear all those great things about her son, and that to this day, I remain his favorite boss.

This experience reminded me of a lesson Lily Star, a Landmark Education course leader, had once shared with me.

> "Your life is a story. And that story is made up of the conversations you most commonly have with those around you. If you change the conversation, you change the story."

The next time I recalled the experience of closing my business, I didn't ruminate on all the problems, issues, or failures. Instead, my thoughts focused on the people with whom I'd worked and our shared stories and experiences. Physically, I noticed myself smiling rather than frowning when I thought about it. It was as if I rewired my brain to think and feel differently.

I shared this story with Spencer, one of my past sales reps who had become a good friend. He decided to try it out himself.

Spencer was ready to quit his job at a tech startup in Boston, but he felt horrible doing it. He had become very close with several people, especially the owners of the company. Spencer felt like he'd be letting everyone down by quitting.

In preparation for deciding to leave, he took the time to write 11 thank you notes to the people he felt closest to in the company. Similarly, in Spencer's notes he reflected on funny stories and great experiences they shared together. He expressed to each person how much he appreciated them and their relationship, regardless of his transition out of the company.

After writing those 11 cards, Spencer told me that his fears and concerns were replaced with feelings of joy and gratitude. His departure from the company wasn't that painful after all.

On a side note, because Spencer handled everything the way he did, his company offered him a part-time consulting role during the transition to his next opportunity. They weren't happy to lose him, but they were happy to support him into the next phase of his career.

## Get Started Today:

Upon reflection, what disempowering stories from your past are still affecting you? What are the gifts in this experience? Who was involved? Who helped you through it? Which relationships have improved and how have you grown because of it?

What might it be like if you brought gratitude to this experience? What letters could you write acknowledging a mistake you made that would initiate self-forgiveness? Or what letters can you write to people to change the conversation?

# Notes to Self

After writing several peace cards, I began to feel a greater sense of peace in my life.

As a result, I wanted to explore more of the message I heard several months ago in the desert: "Heal yourself. Heal the world."

Eager for some fresh perspective, I returned to Dr. Michael, the meditation guru, and shared with him all the breakthroughs I'd experienced by writing peace cards and closing the loop on past relationships. "It's changing my life," I told him, and I wanted to understand why and discover how else I could apply this newfound wisdom.

Dr. Michael said to me, "Internal-emotional pain is healed when we bring love to it. However, when someone is in pain, before they can be open to accepting our love, they must be able to trust us, and if we have hurt them, we must begin by apologizing and owning the breakdown. Only then will the transmittance of love be accepted and people can move forward with their lives."

He asked me, "Have you written any cards to yourself yet?" "No," I replied.

"I encourage you to not just write cards to yourself," he went on, "but to the parts of yourself that are in pain. Think back to specific ages you were when you experienced trauma or serious emotional pain, or disconnection, or the feeling you didn't belong. Imagine yourself at that age and write one of these peace cards to that version of yourself.

"Apologize to that version of yourself for having had to go through that experience. Then bring love to him. Share with him that no matter what happened, he is loved and valued. He is OK. He will be OK, as here you are today.

"Then set an empty chair in front of you and imagine that small child, or adolescent boy sitting there, and read this note. Feel all the feelings that come up, and feel the love you have to give to that part of yourself. Then see what happens."

While I was willing to try some crazy stuff in the name of the Mr. Thank You Project, this was another level beyond my comfort zone.

There were several painful life experiences to speak to, many of which happened when I was very young, specifically stemming from something that happened when I was 13.

I was molested by a close friend at a sleepover.

I was confused, afraid, and ashamed. I didn't want anyone to find out.

It was an experience I never shared with anyone until I met my wife 10 years later. Sadly, I thought I'd be seen as damaged and weak. Of course that's not what happened.

I decided to write my 13-year-old self this note.

I then sat a chair across from myself and imagined that frightened, ashamed,

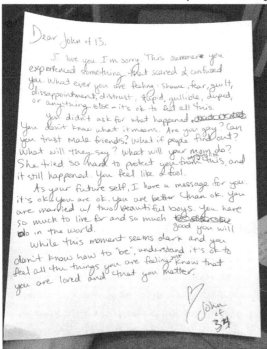

depressed little kid. I had the conversation with him that I wished someone had had with me at that time. Through my letter, I gave him hope, I gave him peace, most importantly I gave him love and allowed him to be.

I then switched seats into the chair that represented that little boy. I closed my eyes and imagined being him again. I allowed myself to feel what I felt back then, the embarrassment, the shame, the guilt—but this time I was also able to feel the love I was able to give him with that letter.

My body began to get physically hot like I was burning off the emotional pain. Afterward, I felt like I had just spent an hour intensely working out at the gym. I felt drained, so I got up, drank some water, and lay down.

I didn't realize the impact of this experience immediately, but I noticed myself being able to more comfortably talk about it if the scenario presented itself.

Eight months after reading myself this letter, I met a woman at a conference who shared with me a struggle she was having with the sexual abuse she received from an ex-boyfriend.

Without hesitation, I shared with her the story of what I went through as a 13-year-old and related to her pain.

She said, "You talk about it with such calm and resilience. How did you get yourself to this place?"

It was at this moment that I saw how powerful this "note to self" was, and the impact of bringing love, gratitude, and acceptance to that terrified little boy who still lived inside of me. I won't say that it healed me completely, but it did open the door to the healing process. It gave a very sad, scared, and pained version of myself some space to breath.

Writing and reading this letter changed my life, and while I have to admit that I am not a psychotherapist and I cannot condone that this will cure all emotional trauma, I can only share with you my own experience. Take with it what you will.

All I can say is that I am grateful for having learned the practice of writing notes to myself, and for the light it has brought to dark spaces in my life.

## Get Started Today:

I will tread lightly with this exercise because some people have some serious experiences or traumas for which they are better off seeing a clinical psychologist.

You also need to be at a place where you are ready to move past this experience. If you are not ready, do not force it.

What I will suggest here is to take a time in your life when you have a lot of pain attached to an experience. Write a letter from the version of you now to that version of yourself back then. Bring love and peace to this version of you. Include the knowledge and awareness you have now from your life experiences to bring perspective and purpose, and if you are able to, share the gift(s) that have come from it.

Get in a quiet place where you won't be interrupted, and you can allow yourself to cry if need be. Read the card to yourself and bring a lot of love and compassion. Forgive yourself, if need be.

Then switch chairs, sit down, and experience all the emotions you had back then. It's OK to cry, it's OK to scream, it's OK to yell. It's also OK to be completely silent. Then, allow yourself to feel the love, acceptance, peace, and wisdom of your current self.

When you are done, journal about it. This is not a quick fix, and we aren't looking for complete and total healing immediately. This is merely starting the healing process to allow all of you to be loved, honored, and respected as you deserve to be.

# Zag-Nation

To not end this section on such a heavy note, I will share with you a story that always makes me smile.

I am not much of a sports guy, unless it deals with my alma mater Gonzaga University and its prolific NCAA men's basketball team.

With under 5,000 undergraduate students, it's remarkable that our team has made it to the last 20 straight NCAA March Madness tournaments, an honor reserved for the top 25 teams in the nation and the champions of each respective conference.

2017 was our year of dominance. We missed a nearly undefeated season with a loss on our home court to Brigham Young University. But all was well: The NCAA tournament was what really mattered at the end of the season.

We squeaked by some close games and beat some really tough teams. For the first time in school history, we made it to the National Championship game against the University of North Carolina.

It was an intense and physical game, and sadly, in the end, my Gonzaga Bulldogs lost.

I've heard of sports enthusiasts getting upset at the loss of a big game, but never have I felt so depressed as I did that night. I felt sick to my stomach. We were so close to being the national champions, but we lost.

The game finished around 9 p.m., and I still had all five cards to write, and honestly, the last thing I wanted to do was be grateful for anything.

As I sat at my desk for a little while, allowing the emotional dust to settle, I thought about how distraught I was feeling. Then I asked myself that ever-guiding question: "How can I bring gratitude to this experience?"

Suddenly, it hit me! *Change the conversation, change the story.*

We didn't lose the National Championship. We went further than any Gonzaga basketball team in our school's history. That deserved celebration!

I decided to write a thank you card to every member of the Gonzaga men's basketball team.

In an instant, after shifting my focus from the pain of the loss to the gift of the big picture, my emotional state did a complete one-eighty.

I found the team roster online, went through every player's stats, and thanked them for the extraordinary season they had played. I noted the games where some had their best performances ever. I acknowledged key games where they were a difference-maker. I pointed out for the "redshirts" that top performance teams come from top performance practices, and if it weren't for their helping prepare the team, we wouldn't have gotten as far as we did.

All in all, I sent 18 cards, including one to the head coach, Mark Few. I also included a copy of my first book *Skating Through College*, which was something I wrote during a time when I guest lectured at colleges and universities.

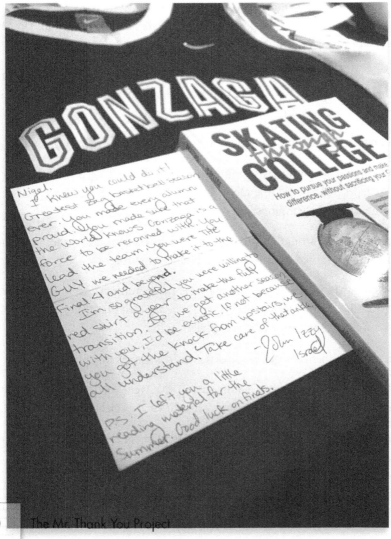

What blew me away was the near immediate transformation that occurred in my emotional state from writing those cards. Whether it was the sports commentators talking about Gonzaga's loss, or friends posting about it on Facebook, I felt no upset, only joy. It was as though my brain just decided to see the loss differently.

Culturally, we often hear the benefits of having a positive mental attitude. We've been encouraged to "look on the bright side" of things, or to seek "the silver lining" during difficult times.

What surprises people when they meet me is that I'll be the first to admit I'm not a naturally positive person. Few of us are. In fact, a majority of our culture has what psychologists call a **negativity bias**.

A negativity bias essentially means that, when presented with equal intensity, negative things have a greater impact on our lives than positive things.

Rick Hanson, Ph.D., is a psychologist, and Senior Fellow of the Greater Good Science Center at UC Berkeley. He explains the negativity bias in his "carrot and stick" analogy.

The carrot is what we want, while the stick is what we want to avoid. We take all actions in our lives because they either bring us closer to pleasure or away from pain, and we are more attracted to avoiding pain than seeking pleasure.

Dr. Hanson explains it this way: "If you miss a carrot today, you'll have the chance to look for one tomorrow. But if you fail to avoid a stick today—WHAP!—no more carrots forever. Compared to carrots, sticks have more urgency and impact."

What does this mean? Our brains are wired to be more attracted to seeing the negative side of a situation more quickly and intensely than to find the positive side. This was great news because I used to feel bad that I couldn't just change my attitude at a moment's notice when faced with a negative situation. Evolutionarily, we just aren't wired that way.

What I was learning during the Mr. Thank You Project is that it's OK to get upset or be annoyed and frustrated. The challenge became not "How do I stop from getting upset?" but "How quickly can I shift from a negative state to a positive or neutral state?"

Asking the question, "How can I bring gratitude to this experience or situation?" proved very helpful in dealing with the National Championship loss of my Gonzaga Bulldogs.

Here's the end of that story.

As with many of the cards I write, I didn't hear anything for a while. But it didn't matter. I was just proud of my Zags and had moved on from the experience.

I all but forgot about the cards I had written until one day, on my birthday of all days, a card showed up from the Gonzaga Men's Basketball Department.

My heart pounded as I opened the envelope. "No flippin' way," I thought to myself. It was handwritten by none other than Mark Few himself, head coach of the Gonzaga Bulldogs.

In his note, Coach Few thanked me for the time I spent to acknowledge and appreciate the entire team. He shared his pride in the players and his gratitude for fans and alumni like me.

While I had received many thank you cards from people who received cards from me or heard about the Mr. Thank You Project, this one was very special.

Coach Few's card symbolized an important lesson. Communities are built through shared experiences and we value those that hold the stance of hope and gratitude during challenging times.

While the Mr. Thank You Project was a large investment of time and energy, it was cards like Coach Few's that fueled me to keep going every day.

I am grateful for my communities.

Life is G

UNITED STATES
POSTAL SERVICE

SANTA "THANK YOU" CLAUS
1 THANK YOU DR.
GRATEFUL, FL 12345

JOHN

OT BEND

# GRATITUDE & COMMUNITY

thank you

"Small acts, **when multiplied by millions of people,** can transform the world."

–Howard Zinn

The Mr. Thank You Project

# Gratitude Creates Community

In the movie, *I Love You, Man*, actor Paul Rudd plays the character, Peter Klaven, a recently engaged man. As he prepares for his wedding, Peter realizes that, aside from his brother and dad, he has no male friends to be part of his side of the wedding party.

The rest of the movie follows Peter as he ventures out into the world, awkwardly trying to make "guy friends" and going on "man-dates" to try and find a best man. It's a funny movie and, sadly, I relate to the entire thing.

After college, I moved back home to San Diego. Very soon after, Monica and I met and started dating long-distance as she lived five hours north in Ventura, California.

I pursued our relationship further by uprooting myself to be closer to her. By that time, I was so engaged with work, and my future with Monica, that I never sought any male relationships.

When Monica and I got engaged, I did have a best man. His name was Nick, my best friend from high school and college.

Nick wanted to throw me a bachelor party, and asked, "Who would you like me to invite?" That's when I felt the same pain as Peter Klaven. Outside of Nick, I didn't really have male friends.

My bachelor party wound up being just me and Nick driving back to San Diego for a night that was supposed to symbolize my transition from bachelor to married man, but in actuality was more symbolic to the state of my male relationships, or lack thereof.

But it didn't get better. After getting married, we started our family, and then moved away to Dallas.

It was at this point that Monica and I set an intention to build our community. And it was also at this time that I started my Mr. Thank You Project.

While the Mr. Thank You Project was proving impactful in my business relationships, and in reconnecting with people from my past, I wanted to see if I could use the project to intentionally build better male relationships.

# The Gratitude Triangle

Of all my many associations, the Front Row Dads community is one that I truly value participating with and contributing to.

Six months after the first event in Philadelphia (remember the pilots and waitress stories?), the Front Row Dads decided to host an event in Austin, Texas.

I had a great time at the first event and wanted to do something extra special, maybe even a little crazy, to deepen the community of the Front Row Dads while in Austin.

At this point, six months into the Mr. Thank You Project, I was all about experiments and tests.

One thing that I realized about the Front Row Dads, like anything with a membership list, is that you have attrition.

What I realized is that it can be difficult to pull men away from their jobs and their families for four days. I know because I experienced this myself. As a parent, when one of the spouses is out of town, that makes extra work for the one at home with the kids.

I was just imagining how many of these men wanted to come back and attend Austin, but would have to revisit the conversation with their spouses about them being gone for several days and all the encompassing responsibilities their wives would be left with.

While this is far from a party, it's easy to understand how some of the wives would be resistant, especially since many of the men are entrepreneurs and travel a lot as it is.

Here's what I decided to do.

With every man that I met in the Austin Front Row Dads Retreat, I asked him one simple question: "What do you love about your wife?"

That question was a powerful one because I'd see these men, often very alpha in nature, soften up as they reflected on what they love about their spouses. It was a great way to get to know each of the men and their families, and it created instant connection.

After every few conversations, I'd grab my journal and make note of the wife's name and what the husband loved about her.

When the Austin Front Row Dads Retreat was over, I grabbed my thank you cards and started writing. While I did send a note to each of the guys, appreciating their attendance at the event, I also decided to write a thank you note to each man's wife.

I called this the gratitude triangle. Writing a thank you card to someone, on behalf of someone else.

What's unique about doing this with a couple is that, as we discussed during the retreat, most men have difficulty being vulnerable and expressing their feelings. It goes against the image of being a strong male figure who needs to "hold it together." We are not very practiced in expressing our emotions.

Another reality is that, the longer people are married, the more likely they are to take their spouses for granted, and we fail to acknowledge and appreciate them for the things that have just become natural routine.

Now I know what you're thinking, "How would it look for a man to write another man's wife a thank you card?"

I'd be lying to say I wasn't nervous. I thought, "This is going to be either really good, or really bad. Either way, it'll make for a great story."

Here's an example of what I wrote to 30+ wives from the Front Row Dads Retreat:

Hi _____,

It might be odd to receive a thank you note from someone you've never met, but I spent a few days getting to know your husband at the Front Row Dads Retreat in Austin, Texas.

I am sending you this card because as a husband, I understand that when I leave for trips like this, my wife's workload doubles with the kids. It probably wasn't easy to have your husband gone for this trip, but I just want to thank you for all you do to support him. The event was tremendous, and your husband's participation was really valued.

When he and I were talking, I asked, What do you love about your wife? His eyes lit up and he shared how much he loves (insert husband's comments here). Ex.

−Your commitment to your family's faith

−How compassionate you are with the twins when they don't get along

−The way you always make sure the coffee is ready when he wakes up

−Your passion for the business you run and the example you are for your girls

Hopefully, our families will get to meet one day. But until then, thank you for all you do, and we wish the best for your family this coming summer. God bless.

−John Israel

Each note was personalized with what their husband shared with me, so that part was different every time. The husbands had no idea I planned to do this, though they might have wondered why I emailed them asking for their home mailing addresses.

Such is the life of Mr. Thank You. Either way, they obliged, and I sent the letters.

Over the next few weeks, I received email after email from husbands telling me how much those cards meant to them and their wives. Many said their wives cried when they read them, and others' husbands raved about all the "brownie points" it scored them.

One particular wife sent me a personal handwritten note saying, "You're right. Being a mother isn't easy. We love our husbands, so we do it anyway. It's great to know he's coming back with such value and I'm grateful he's getting to meet awesome dads like you."

This was the exact reaction I was looking for.

Fast forward another six months, in October 2017 at the end of my year-long gratitude project, we had another Front Row Dads Retreat in Santa Cruz, California. While we were on the beach, several of the husbands commented on how impactful it was for me to have sent those notes to their wives and how their wives now look forward to these retreats.

If my mission was to develop more male relationships with the Mr. Thank You Project, this one act accomplished that goal.

While I haven't always been a great friend, there is at least one important rule I've learned: Friendship is about having each other's back.

The most important relationship to a married person is with his or her spouse. If being a friend to you means that my most important relationship gets better, then you are a good friend to have.

# Communal Gratitude Experience

Communal gratitude experiences are when a community gets together to send love and appreciation to a specific person or small group of people. Oftentimes this person is underappreciated or undervalued.

Now that I had practiced building community with gratitude, I wanted to practice giving communities the opportunity to participate in the Mr. Thank You Project.

On a simple scale, when I'd write a thank you card to a waiter or waitress, I'd invite everyone at my table to sign the note or write a comment.

It was fun. It didn't matter for me to get credit or for me to experience someone's reaction to a card. Now I loved watching other people get involved.

However, I wanted to take it up a notch.

At month eight, I was on a trip to Philadelphia to deliver a presentation about Mr. Thank You. Another presenter I became friends with on the trip was named Jeff Kaylor.

Jeff is a magician based out of Orlando, Florida, and he has a remarkable program where he performs magic and delivers keynote messages teaching audiences how to create "magic moments" for people they care about.

One of the things that stuck out about Jeff's message was something that he calls, "Conspiracy Theory."

Conspiracy Theory is when several people are in on a secret to surprise someone else. That secret is something that bonds that group or community and heightens the experience of surprise for the receiver.

This is why surprise parties are so fun. While it's a remarkable experience for the receiver, it's also exciting for those who participate.

Jeff gave examples of inviting friends to his house. Before their arrival, Jeff would reach out to that friend's closest family to get pictures and all sorts of data that would be fun to know or play on.

The friend would walk in to their guest room at Jeff's house and, on the nightstand would be family photos from the friend's childhood. Their favorite candy laid out on the bed, and their favorite song would be playing on the stereo.

Elaborate, no? Did this elevate the experience of the guest? Absolutely. Did it excite the friends and family who helped Jeff pull it off? You know it.

Inspired by Jeff's ideas, I wondered, "How can I incorporate this into the Mr. Thank You Project?"

# 30,000 Feet of Gratitude

On June 6th, 2017, I had a long five-hour flight from Philadelphia to Las Vegas. I decided to push the envelope yet again.

I travel a lot and by this point I had already written nearly 20 thank you cards to pilots on my planes. I thought, "This is such a fun thing for me, but I want other people to experience it."

As we boarded the plane, I did my usual part, finding out the pilots' names, but after takeoff, I also found out the names of the three flight attendants on board serving us.

I took out five thank you cards, and I wrote a shorter, simpler note than usual to each of the pilots and flight attendants. But this time I embarked on a communal twist.

I put the letters in a brown folder, and I attached a sticky note with instructions on what to do. Essentially, I invited everyone on the plane to participate in the Mr. Thank You Project by writing a note of appreciation for each of the pilots and flight attendants. They did not have to join in, but I requested they still pass the folder on to the next passenger. I also asked that this be done secretly, keeping it from the flight attendants, as I didn't want them to find out and spoil the fun.

Now, I was in the middle of this plane, and sitting next to me was a woman in a red dress. I instructed the last person on the plane to give the folder to her so as not to draw any attention to myself. I wanted this to be anonymous, but if they needed to give someone a "wink" on the way to the bathroom, I preferred it be my neighbor. Who knows what the red dress woman thought?

I walked to the front of the plane to a row of three lovely senior women and explained the project. It was a funny sight because they were a little hard of hearing, plus I had to overcome the sound of the engine, so I was practically yelling the instructions to them, but hopefully not so loud that the flight attendant caught on. The women agreed it was a beautiful idea and would gladly participate.

I walked back to my seat with three and a half hours of flight time in front of me.

Tick. Tick. Tick. Thirty minutes went by, and I didn't see anything being passed around. My internal dialog started racing.

*You crossed the border this time. This is too weird.*

*Why are you doing this?*

*What if no one signs the cards and it's a complete failure? What if they report you to TSA?*

*You are going to get kicked off the plane.*

*You'll go to jail.*

*You'll never fly again.*

*Ahhhh ...*

Then I saw the brown folder pass over someone's head five rows from the front. "OK, OK. It's coming along," I told myself.

I was so excited and nervous that I couldn't read a book, listen to music, or work on my laptop. I could only sit there and wait with anticipation.

I saw the folder passed and passed and passed, and then it finally got to me. I opened it up and ... oh, my God. Signatures and notes of appreciation everywhere. It was totally working!

But there was a problem. The cards were nearly full, and we were only halfway through the flight. I added my pad of sticky notes with the folder, saying, "Use these if you run out of room."

Tick. Tick. Tick. Thirty minutes before landing, I decided to go to the restroom in the rear of the plane and check on the folder. I found it on the second-to-last row. "Oh, my goodness," I thought. "We're actually pulling this off."

I headed back to my seat, excited to receive the folder.

Unfortunately, the pilot called for landing preparations, so no one could get up—but that wasn't a problem. I would just wait for the person in the last row to get off, and then I'd grab the folder (in lieu of the woman in red).

The plane landed and people began to exit. I stood in my aisle with a big, cheesy grin, waiting for the last person to come through. But ... nothing. No one handed me the folder.

"Where the heck are my thank you cards?" I asked myself.

Now, this plane was also heading to another destination, so several people were still on the plane in their original seats, and the people in the last row were still sitting there.

"OK, they must have it," I thought to myself.

I walked back and asked, "Hey, did you see that brown folder come by?"

"Folder?" asked the passenger. "Oh yeah, the brown one. I handed it to the flight attendant."

"Bah … surprise foiled," I thought. I was hoping to be the one to give it to them.

I walked up to the flight attendant and asked, "Hey, did someone give you a brown folder?"

The flight attendant replied, "Folder? Folder? Oh yes, I was going around collecting trash, and someone handed it to me. I threw it away. It's in the trash truck over there." He points out the window to the small truck parked on the runway.

My heart sank.

"You *have* to get that folder!" I pleaded. "It has thank you cards signed by everyone on this plane."

"Oh my gosh, are you serious?" asked the flight attendant.

Without hesitation, he ran down the stairs to the trash truck just before it pulled away. The trash man had to remove his headphones to hear what the erratic flight attendant was saying. They both pulled all the trash bags off the truck, ripping them open and scattering cups, magazines, and trash everywhere.

I stood there in disbelief as, at last, the flight attendant pulled out the brown folder of thank you cards. However, the folder was drenched in water, wine, soda, and who knows what else.

With sunken shoulders and sadness on his face, the flight attendant walked back up the stairs toward me.

He handed me the folder, and said, "I'm so sorry sir. I had no idea what was in here." I sat down in a chair to take a moment and assess the damage.

When I opened the folder, inside were all five cards in perfect condition—in fact, better than perfect condition. Every square inch of every card was filled with passengers' signatures and notes of appreciation. Sticky notes lined the entire inside of the folder.

Now my heart wanted to explode.

Before I could get too wrapped up in the moment, I had to respect that this plane was about to board new passengers, so I needed to quickly get out of there.

I frantically grabbed my phone to take a few photos to document this insane experience. Then I piled the sticky notes into their respective cards, shoved them into their envelopes, and handed them out to each flight attendant and pilot.

At this point my cover was blown. As I exited the plane, it became evident to everyone still aboard: I am Mr. Thank You.

As I walked up the aisle, someone stopped me and said, "Was that you who started that whole thank you card thing?"

"Yes," I replied.

"That was one of the most extraordinary experiences I've ever been a part of. Thank you for involving us."

A few rows later, a father stopped me to say, "Thank you for doing this. My 8-year-old son was sitting next to me as your folder showed up. As we wrote in the cards together, it gave me an opportunity to explain the importance of kindness and appreciation."

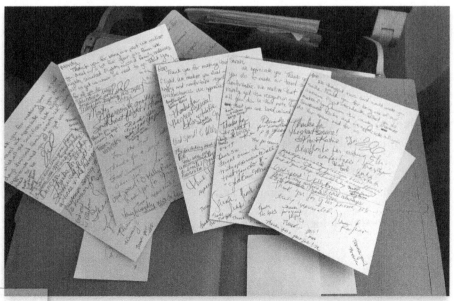

While I didn't get to sit there and watch the reactions of the pilots and flight attendants as they read their cards, I was able to learn one of the most important lessons of the Mr. Thank You Project.

When we give up the need to receive credit, the value and impact of an experience multiplies. While I got to have a great story to tell, everyone got to leave with the memory of that experience. And I'm sure it was pretty cool for the pilots and flight attendants as well.

While I didn't know how, I knew it was time to expand the Mr. Thank You Project on a global scale.

## Get Started Today:

Before you jump on an airplane with a box of thank you cards, there are many other great ways to create your own communal gratitude experience.

We have seen classrooms of students do this for a teacher. Players on sports teams do it for their coaches or assistant coaches.

Think of someone in your life or work who works extremely hard, yet is rarely recognized for it. Privately organize a group of people via email, text message, or word of mouth to write a handwritten card for this person. Invite them to share how much they love and appreciate this specific person. Maybe include a story of how they improved your life or made you laugh one day.

Pick a designated day or time to drop off the cards at a specific location. Give the cards to that person at a specific event or meeting, and prepare a short speech about why this person matters so much to everyone. Then surprise the person.

If you'd prefer to keep it more private, you can decorate the person's desk or room with the notes.

Another way to produce a communal gratitude experience for a loved one is on their birthday. Reaching out to their friends and family with a note or email inviting them to write a letter with similar content as above, but sent it on a specific date. This way your loved one will get one or multiple cards in the mail every day leading up to and including the person's birthday, and even after. Watch as they put two and two together to realize you are the one behind it all.

Important note: Make sure to appreciate all the people who took the time to send in a note so they know the impact of their efforts.

# The Birth of a Movement

"Check it out. I started making my own thank you cards."

Nick, a stranger before the Mr. Thank You Project, but a good friend by the end, showed me this amazing thank you card he had designed after he was inspired by the project.

Nick was a member of the Front Row Dads, and after I sent him a thank you card from our first interaction, he sent me one back. We had to joke that at some point someone needs to stop sending a thank you card for a thank you card.

One day, Nick and I got together and he showed me these amazing thank you cards he had designed with sayings and words that inspired him. He sent these thank you cards to friends, family, mentors, and leaders he appreciated in his life.

"How many have you sent out?" I asked him. "Over 100," he replied.

I was blown away and congratulated him on his efforts.

When I asked Nick what he had gotten from his own Mr. Thank You Project, he said, "A deeper connection to those I send a card to. A rich understanding of authenticity and what it means/feels like to be me."

He even received a consulting offer from a woman to whom he sent a card.

At the end of our conversation, Nick said, "It would be cool if you had a website that tracked all the thank you cards you are inspiring. I can't be the only one doing this."

He was right. Every week I'd get a thank you note, email, or Facebook message from someone who started writing thank you cards as a daily practice. Some were going for 30-day challenges, others were attempting to write one card every day for the year, and everywhere in between.

I don't know the first thing about building a website, so I consulted my good friend and tech wizard, Spencer Dixon, about building a prototype. In one month's time he had it up and running.

While it was simple, it worked.

People could go to the website, type in their name, email, and how many cards they sent. As soon as they hit enter, our global gratitude number would increase. It was exciting to go to the website and see that number grow every week.

Unfortunately, we didn't have a way to stop false numbers from being submitted, and one day our thank you card count escalated to 200,000,000. Either we finally hit a tipping point and inspired global change, or some jokester was taking advantage of the fact that we had no filter or authentication process. I assume the latter.

While it took several months, several other developers, and several thousands of dollars of my personal savings, we came out with a version that was more robust and secure.

This is the platform from which we are building the movement.

A snapshot of www.MrThankYou.com

Nick's Card

# THE ROI OF GRATITUDE

"All things being equal, people will do business with, and refer business to, those people they know, like, and trust."

–*Bob Burg*

# Assuming the Best in People

About 15 years before the Mr. Thank You Project, when I was a mere 19-year-old Cutco salesperson, I finished a sales call with a wonderful woman who purchased a modest order of knives. Her name was Cindy.

We had such a great time together that I'd have enjoyed her company even if she hadn't bought anything.

Unfortunately, 48 hours after the appointment, I received a call from the woman, and her tone was somber. She needed to cancel her order.

Shocked, I asked if there was something I did or said, or if there was something I could do or say for her to keep the order. She said, "Something came up. And I don't know if or when I will be buying Cutco."

I could tell she didn't want to talk about it, so I pulled back and wished her well.

A few days later, I noticed myself still thinking about the woman and the great time we had together, so I decided to write her a thank you note, appreciating her for our time together. In a nutshell, I said:

> *Dear Cindy,*
>
> *Thank you for your time the other day. I really enjoyed visiting with you, talking and learning about your kids and your family. I realize that right now is not the time for you to purchase any Cutco, and that's fine. I just wanted you to know I had a great time regardless. You are a hard-working single mom who cares deeply about her family. I'm so glad your friend introduced us. If there's anything I can do to serve you down the line, please do not hesitate to contact me.*
>
> *—John*

I sent the note and remember feeling really good about the decision. Regardless of our business transaction, I was just grateful to have met her.

Three years later, I received a call from a familiar voice. She said, "Is this Cutco John?" "Yes," I replied.

"This is your old client Cynthia Blackman. Do you remember me?" "Of course. How are you?"

"Well, I'm doing much better and am ready to buy some Cutco knives from you finally."

Shocked, I then helped Cynthia purchase an order three times the size of the original.

Before we finished the phone call, she said, "You know, John, all those years ago when I had to cancel my order with you, I felt terrible. What I couldn't tell you is I was diagnosed with cancer. Being a single mother, I had to leave my job and take care of myself. My boys moved back in with me to help out. Life was rough for a while.

"The card you sent me meant so much. Once I got healthy and went back to work, I knew I wanted to order some Cutco knives from you. That's why I'm calling you today."

My heart melted.

In the moment of writing Cindy that card all those years ago, I had no ulterior motive. I had no expectation that she would ever get in touch with me again. I just wanted to treat her with the respect she deserved.

I distinctly remember thinking, "How would I want a salesperson to treat my own mother?"

Instead of assuming the worst, what if we believed the best in people? It's not what we do or say, but how we make people feel that most encourages them to do business with us again.

# The ROI of Gratitude

I often speak at conferences and on podcasts on the topic of gratitude as it relates to business and career success. Invariably, all the business people want to know is, "What's the ROI (Return On Investment)? Have you seen any direct monetary benefit from this Mr. Thank You Project?"

Before answering that question, I realize that some people reading this book are not directly in business or might be turned off with this topic of benefits one might gain from intentionally expressing gratitude. But before you throw the baby out with the bathwater I want you and everyone else to understand something:

## If you attempt to use gratitude for the sole purpose of monetary, business, or personal gain, it will cause more harm than good.

Genuine gratitude and appreciation is pure in nature. If we approach people with the intent to "get something," we negate the act of writing thank you cards in the first place.

Not only will the individual be turned off by those actions, but you will miss out on the most significant benefits of the authentic appreciation: living gratefully.

The greatest gift you will receive from writing thank you cards, as we've discussed in this book, is that YOU will become more grateful from the process.

If you make thank you cards a habit in your business or organization, whether it be sending cards to clients, prospects, or even people who take their business elsewhere, you are training your brain to value people at a higher level. Customers are no longer just numbers. They are people. They are someone's brother, sister, mother, father, son, or daughter. The more cards I wrote, the more present I was to the "humanness" of people, rather than their dollar value.

That being said, even if you are not in business, nor do you have the desire to be in business one day, you might find this section interesting as it can give you more insight into companies or organizations that you care about and how the habit of writing thank you cards can have a transformative effect on their progress and engagement with the communities they serve.

So, did I receive direct monetary benefit from writing five thank you cards every day for a year? Yes.

But before we dive into that, let's talk about the costs.

## Financial:

As nice an idea as it was to write 1,825 thank you cards in a year, it wasn't free.

Here were some of the hard costs:

2,000 cards: approximately $.75 each = $1,500

*(Some cards I discarded, and I also wrote closer to 1,850 cards for the year, some days writing more than five in a day, as well as people who received more than three for the year and therefore did not count toward the challenge.)*

1,850 stamps: $.49 each = $906.50

*(This is an estimate. Some cards did not need a stamp, as I handed them directly to recipients (waitresses or pilots, for instance). Others, however, were international, and in some cases I sent the card with a book, which cost three times as much as postage.)*

Miscellaneous supplies (pens, address stampers, custom rubber stamps, etc.):

= approximately $100. Grand total: $2,506.50.

Depending on your values and beliefs, that might seem like a lot of money; to others, not so much. The real question is, did writing that many thank you cards actually generate more than $2,506.50 in value or income?

Short answer: Yes.

## Direct Income Reflection:

When you are in business, whether small or big, every dollar matters. As the old adage goes, "If it doesn't make dollars, it doesn't make sense."

In one week alone, I had two clients call to place orders directly because of their thank you cards. Those orders generated an additional $2,300 in commissions.

While it was nice to see a direct correlation when a client called and mentioned the thank you card, not everyone did. It was hard to measure 100 percent of that income effect.

However, one interesting fact that we could measure was the reduction in canceled business.

## Reduction in Cancellations:

Every company, business, or organization deals with retention issues. Every product has a cancellation or return rate. Churches have a percentage of people who come to church for one service and never come back again. Colleges have a percent of students who attend freshman year and not their sophomore.

Some of those retention rates are as small as .01 percent, while others expect 20-30-50 percent or more of people won't come back, follow through, or keep the product they purchased.

I have a friend in solar sales that expects 20 percent of the contracts signed to fall through before the panels are scheduled for install. With the size of commissions a solar installation creates, that's equivalent to $10,000+ of income a sales rep loses throughout the year.

My return or cancellation rate hovered between 3-5 percent throughout my career. Meaning out of every 100 clients I'd work with, 3-5 would cancel or return their orders.

During the Mr. Thank You Project, my cancellation rate dropped to 1.7 percent. Now this difference may not seem like a large amount, but that number is nearly 50 percent lower than my best cancellation rate. In hard numbers, that equivocated to $5,470 in income saved from noncancelled sales.

This was the number that really struck me, because nothing had changed in my selling process. The only thing that changed was my follow-up.

At the end of every day, I'd look through the clients I had closed a transaction with and write them thank you notes.

In the notes I acknowledged anything particular that I enjoyed from our conversation, whether it be a discussion about the family, a vacation, or a hobby. I took the time to appreciate their trust in doing business with me as they had a lot of options in the industry. Lastly, I expressed that if they had any questions or problems, they could call me directly.

This last part was what I believed to be the difference-maker. There were several clients who, for whatever reason, had a concern or a question that would normally result in a cancellation. However, instead of returning their products, they'd call me to flesh out their problems. Most of the time, I answered their concerns and they kept their orders.

For others, it was better for them to simply cancel.

The distinction I saw from this occurrence was that people appeared to have a higher level of trust with me such that they felt comfortable reaching out with any concerns.

While this might seem like a strange stat to share in this book, think of it this way:

*Money you don't lose is money you make.*

While I can't claim a guaranteed 50 percent reduction in cancellations across the board for everyone else, it does bring up an interesting question: How can companies and organizations involve gratitude as a practice to retain clients, employees, or participants?

Organizational leaders are astounded by these numbers and intrigued by the potential because they understand the shift that small changes can have on a large scale.

Again, I walk a fine line here of not encouraging people to "use" gratitude as a way to get something.

What I have found is that most people I talk to already know that writing thank you cards is a good thing to do, but they are just too busy to do it. However, when these same people see that it's not a reduction in their time, but an investment in their relationships AND has a direct return, they start looking for opportunities to incorporate gratitude into their processes.

# Delegating Gratitude

Many associates I know have implemented thank you cards into different parts of their client interaction processes but have delegated the writing to an assistant.

If that's you, I'm not here to say you are a bad person. In fact, I'm not even going to tell you to stop. If it's the difference of never sending a thank you card or having a staff member do it, delegate away. Something is better than nothing, in this case.

However, I also want you to consider the impact or lack thereof.

Have you ever received a thank you card from someone and felt like it was generic? The reaction is commonly, "Oh, they send this to everyone."

The unique power of a handwritten note in today's society is that we all know how much easier it is to send an email, text, or message online. It takes a significant amount of time for someone to find some stationery, write the message, put it in an envelope, find the physical mailing address, put a stamp on the envelope, and drop said letter in the mailbox.

While 50 years ago, mailing a handwritten note was a common way for people to communicate, nowadays we have so many options, no one expects it. This is the exact reason why the impact of a genuine handwritten note is of such high value. We know it takes time, and it causes the receiver to think, consciously or subconsciously, "Wow, they really care about me."

As soon as a client perceives the lack of genuineness from a generic thank you note, it is experienced more as an advertisement than a genuine expression of appreciation.

The client reaction is neutral at best.

A few years before I began the Mr. Thank You Project, I had an assistant helping me write thank you cards.

I pre-wrote sample cards for her based on the client scenario (first-time customer, repeat customer, referral, or trade show lead). When she received the client's order form to process, I included a sticky note identifying the type of client, so she knew what card to write. It was a pretty good system.

In fact, it worked great until a client emailed me to say, "John, congratulations on your business success. I can tell you're doing well because you obviously have someone helping write your thank you cards. They spelled your last name incorrectly on the one they sent me. I only know because she also included your business card inside with the correct spelling."

While I appreciated my client's humor, I also wanted to crawl under a rock and die of embarrassment.

I found out that, for an entire month, my assistant was spelling my last name wrong on every thank you card (It's I-S-R-A-E-L, not I-S-R-E-A-L).

It was about this time that I re-took over the task of writing my own thank you cards.

Here are my thoughts on delegation: If you are going to delegate anything, delegate everything after the writing of the note. You don't have to address, stamp, or mail the letter. That, in fact, was the most time-consuming part of the Mr. Thank You Project. If I could do it over, I would have hired someone purely for the purpose of making sure all my cards were sent out in a timely fashion to the correct locations. No one would consider, or care if it was your handwriting on the outside, but they would care if the contents were from you.

## A Note on Penmanship:

Some people have asked me about penmanship. What if you have horrible writing, or you aren't the best speller? For starters, most people don't care as much about that as you think. Don't let it stop you.

However, if you are still nervous about your handwriting, I recommend that you type the letter in your own words, add something to make it personal so they know it was meant for them and not a "form letter," print it, and sign the letter in blue ink. That way they know it's an original.

There's also a few companies who have online platforms that you can type the card out, including the person's mailing address. The company will print the card, stamp, and mail it for you. SendOutCards is a good company that does this, as well as Bond, and a few others in the market.

# Lead with Gratitude

I remember a story my father shared with me about one of the most meaningful artifacts from his 25-year career with AT&T. As a systems technician, my dad did everything from climbing telephone poles to installing telecommunication systems on Navy battleships.

One time he was flown out to South America to install the communication system on an Army base. The local general to the camp expressed to my father that, politically, times were tense in the country, and my father and his partner were given a tight timeline to complete a large and complex job before a new shipment of soldiers was to arrive.

My dad and his partner worked around the clock to complete their job. While it was an exhilarating and stressful experience, they managed to finish a half-day earlier than contracted.

While they were sitting in their barracks getting packed to come home, an Army personnel walked in and handed my father and his partner a typed, yet hand-signed letter from the general.

In the letter, the general expressed his appreciation for the quick and speedy installation of their telecom systems. This meant the safety and security of American lives on foreign soil, and for that, the general was grateful.

One thing that impacted my father about this letter was that it wasn't expected. In his 25 years of working for AT&T, he had never received a note of appreciation from a client.

He was just "doing his job," as he would say.

The second thing that was so meaningful was the caliber of the man who wrote it.

Power and position can often create a disconnect between people. Individuals in high- level roles have so much important work to do, that something as simple as a personalized note might be considered unnecessary or "below their pay grade." This especially elevates the impact of such a note.

This is why I encourage anyone in leadership, whether they are the CEO, general manager, or head of a church, to take the time to write personal notes of appreciation to people in their organizations. The impact can be profound because people get how important you are and when you take the time to acknowledge them, it carries weight.

While it's more of an investment of time than money, we create loyalty when we create trust. And we create trust when we craft experiences that show our people how much they matter to us.

## Get Started Today:

When you think about your business or organizations that you are involved with, what parts of the client, employee, or user interaction could a handwritten note help to deepen the relationships or create meaningful connections?

Pick five to 10 of these people and practice or test out sending them a personal, handwritten thank you note. Notice two things: How this affects you in your appreciation level for them and make note of their reactions, responses, or how it impacts the organization.

If you feel so called, share your story with us through **www.MrThankYou.com** or in the Facebook community. We love to hear success stories.

# Coming to an End

I'll never forget the phone call when my long-time friend Nick called to tell me that his father had passed away. His father's name was Anthony.

I felt terrible for my friend's loss, and for the missed opportunity to tell his dad how much I appreciated him.

To make matters worse, I had a card for Anthony sitting on my desk that I had written several weeks earlier, but had been "too busy" to send it.

While I wished more than anything that Anthony would have been able to read the card himself, I took a valuable lesson from that experience that affected the intentionality and importance of the Mr. Thank You Project.

If we can tell someone how much we appreciate them, we should. Not tomorrow, but today.

With 7.4 billion people on the planet, every day people die with regrets of things they wish they had said or done. And for every one of those people, there is a family member or friend who wishes they could have just one more conversation with that person that they'll never get to have.

If you knew you would die tomorrow, who would you call first? What would you tell them? Do it.

It's in these questions that we get real about who and what matters most.

Now imagine being at the end of your life, and instead of worrying about who you should call, you can just enjoy the time you have, surrounded by who you love because you've spent your life living wholeheartedly, communicating and expressing how much you value and care for everyone in your life.

What a way to go.

# A Final Note

Before we go, I have one more card to share with you. This is the last card I wrote during my Mr. Thank You Project.

It is the card I had been wanting to write for a long time. It's my thank you card to you, the reader.

While we may not know each other yet, what I know about you is that you are another one of the good ones. Another human being out there committed to making a difference. No one else would read this far in to the book if that wasn't the case.

If this book or project has inspired you in any way, I'd love to know. You can reach out to me directly at John@MrThankYou.com.

Dear Reader,

Come on... are you surprised? Do you think we could spend all this time together and me not write you a "Thank You" card?

You might be wondering, "But John, we don't even know each other. What can you possibly have to Thank me for?"

For starters: Thank you for picking this book up and reading it to the end. You can spend your time doing anything, and I am humbled to know you have taken the time to listen to my story. It means a lot, and I appreciate you for it.

Secondly, I thank you for whatever actions you have taken or are going to take to increase the level of gratitude in your own life and the lives of those around you. Thank you for being courageous. Thank you for being vulnerable. Thank you for being a beacon of light for the world to see of what's possible when you live whole-heartedly expressing love and gratitude for those that matter most. You being <u>you</u> gives others permission to be who <u>they</u> are.

I am grateful and thankful for who you are and all the life experiences that have led you to where you are in this very moment. I am sorry for your pain, and your loss, and the times you felt alone, unloved, or didn't belong. It needed to happen. You are the key to unlocking the transformation in others because you are perfectly imperfect, just like them and that's what they need to know change is possible.

I'll never forget you. I'll never forget this moment. You are the final card in my year of Thank You, and I couldn't imagine it going to anyone better.

Thank you! I love you! You are awesome!

Keep in touch.

Sincerely,

AKA Mr. Thank You

# Call to Action: 30-Day Challenge

I've met several people who, after hearing about the project say, "I love it. I'm going to write five cards a day every day for a year too."

My reaction is, "You don't have to do that many to receive the benefit of making gratitude a habit in your life. Start with one card a day for 30 days and expand from there."

We've found that 30 days is a much more manageable amount to commit and follow through on. You can up the amount per day, but keep it simple for starters. We don't want you getting burnt out on gratitude.

I created a PDF resource you can download at **www.MrThankYou.com/30** on how to start your own 30-Day Mr. (or Miss) Thank You Project.

My only ask is that you let us know how it goes. Make sure to create a profile at **www.MrThankYou.com** so that you can log all your thank you's and track your progress.

Also, make sure to join our Facebook community at **www.Facebook.com/MrThankYou** and share your successes, wins, or challenges.

If you have a company or organization you'd like to get involved in the Mr. Thank You Project, or you have a communal gratitude experience you'd like to create, visit our resource section at **www.MrThankYou.com** for an action plan or tip sheet.

# Frequently Asked Questions

### Did you miss any days?

I did not. The habit became so ingrained in my brain that one night after a long day, I fell asleep at 8:30 p.m. on the couch while attempting to watch television. I was so exhausted that I fell into a deep REM sleep, and in my dream, my wife ran up to me, shook me, and said, "You need to finish your cards."

I awakened instantly to find my wife fast asleep with our kids in bed. When I looked at the clock, it was 11:59 p.m. I finished my cards by 1:30 a.m. and "officially" went to bed.

### Did anything bad or weird ever result from writing all those thank you notes?

Nothing strange or awkward occurred that I'm aware of. Could someone have been weirded out by a thank you card from a stranger? Possibly. If they were, I didn't hear about it, and last time I checked there were no warrants out for a guy who's thanking people too much.

### What cards do you prefer?

I purchased thank you cards from about every available source. I'd go to Target and clean them out. Amazon has a few suppliers with great deals. Paper Source and Papyrus are my favorite cards for special occasions. Of course, we have our own line of Mr. Thank You cards available on our website. No matter who you buy them from, you're on the right track.

### What if I have bad handwriting? Is it OK to type my cards?

If you are self-conscious about your handwriting, typing a letter and hand-signing it can carry the same sentiment.

### Do I have to write five thank you cards every day to participate in the Mr. Thank You Project?

No. You could write only one card and still be a participant. Just make sure to log it on **www.MrThankYou.com**. On our Facebook group, some of the users hold 30-day challenges, and you could partner with them, or even share this book with a friend and partner with them to create your own Mr. Thank You Project.

### Did you continue writing thank you cards every day after the project was complete?

I did continue writing cards, but not every day and not five every day. While I had been spending 90 minutes every day writing cards during the project, I switched that time to writing the book. Now that this book is complete, I'll be organizing more communal gratitude experiences, which are often more time-intensive (and can be pretty dang fun).

# My List

While you heard about many of my recipients throughout the book, there's no way I could talk about every single card I wrote.

Below is a list that encompasses a majority of the people that I wrote thank you cards to. While there are bound to be a few categories I missed, this should give you a good frame of reference for your own journey.

- Assistants
- Associates
- Astronauts
- Authors
- Babysitters
- Baristas
- Best friends from college
- Billing departments
- Clothes
- Clients
- Co-authors
- Co-workers
- College professors
- Corporate staff
- Customer service agents
- Department heads
- Early life heroes
- Employees
- Family
- Flight attendants
- Friends
- Friends' parents
- Friends' spouses
- Governors
- High school teachers
- Homeless people
- Hotel managers
- Hotel maids
- Mayors
- Mentors
- Missionaries
- Park rangers
- Pastors
- People I love
- People I have a hard time loving
- People on Instagram
- People who have provided me opportunities
- People who have passed away
- Pilots
- Potential clients
- Presidents
- Prison inmates
- Professional skateboarders
- Professional speakers
- Prospective clients
- Spouse
- Spouse's friends
- Store managers
- Television producers
- Television show hosts
- The IRS
- Uber drivers
- Utility companies
- Vendors
- Waiters and waitresses
- You

# What's Next?

Our mission is about building community. While our first objective is to inspire 74 million thank you cards written all over the world, we realize that not one person, group, or company can do it on their own. It will take the collective consciousness and efforts of many who care about this mission and see the value of honoring people for their value and gifts in the world.

We want to support people making gratitude a habit.

In alignment with this, we are providing support to organizations, schools, and churches who are starting their own Mr. Thank You groups and projects. Some are using this as an opportunity to appreciate major members inside of their organizations. For others, this is a great opportunity to thank valued vendors or partners who have done much to support. Some are doing outreaches to prison workers, missionaries, volunteer organizations, and more. The list goes on and on.

If you have a story of how this project has impacted, influenced, or changed your life, we want to hear about it.

If you haven't already, go to **www.MrThankYou.com**, create a free user profile, and submit your story.

For any inquiries about interviews, podcasts, speaking engagements, consulting, or partnerships, email: **admin@mrthankyou.com**

And if you need to contact us for any other reason, our updated contact info can be found on our website.

Thank you once again, and God bless. Sincerely,

John Israel Founder

The Mr. Thank You Project

# Acknowledgements

Thank you to my lovely and wonderful wife Monica for all the time and space you created for me to be able to write my cards every day, and then write this book. You are my source of inspiration. Everything I do, I do for you and the boys.

Anderson and Rohn, thank you for making me smile every morning with your genuine enthusiasm. You are what I am grateful for every day I wake up.

My parents, Ron & Kathleen Israel, for teaching me my faith and all the lessons I never thanked you for until I was much later in life. I am who I am because of you. Also, thank you to my siblings Lisa, Peter, Carla, & Cecilia for being the best brothers and sisters I could have asked for.

To all the family, aunts, uncles, cousins, nieces, and nephews. May the Donnelly and Israel Legacies live on with you.

To my buddy Spencer Dixon for building out the first Mr. Thank You website simply because I thought it would be a great idea. Thank you Spencer for following your heart and using your gifts to make the world a better place.

John Peterson & David Lesches, my web developers who took my crazy idea to the next level.

To Ben Schemper, Zach Wagner, Jake Merriman, Mike Ambrosino, Justin Janowski, Andrew Biggs and everyone at Epic Impact for your leadership, friendship, and guidance.

Mike McCarthy, Tim Rhode, David Osborn, Rock Thomas, and all the leadership and members of Gobundance. Thank You for your friendship and the opportunity to be a part of and share my message with the tribe.

Lance and Brandy Salazar, Aaron & Kaleena Amuchastegui, Ken & Amber Wimberly and all the members of Fambundance for your commitment to supporting the marriage unit and for your love and contribution to the Israel family.

To Jon Vroman and the Front Row Dad's for being such a source of inspiration in my life and who I am becoming as a man and father.

Hal Elrod & Jon Berghoff for opening doors I could never have opened on my own.

To my mentors and friends, many of whom received cards from me and encouraged the effort of what I was up to. And for any of you I forgot to send a card to, you know I love you too.

# About the author

John Israel, is the founder of The Mr. Thank You Project, a global movement to inspire 74 million thank you cards written all over the world.

John is an author, speaker, and business owner. He speaks at organizational and business conferences all over the world teaching people how they can utilize gratitude through written word to enhance well-being, build community, and grow their bottom line.

John has been featured on ABC News, Fox News, Good Morning America, PopSugar, and MarthaStewart.com for his work on gratitude.

To book John for your event or show, visit our Media/Booking section of www.MrThankYou.com, and place an inquiry.

Made in the USA
Monee, IL
16 August 2021